On Murray's Run

Joe Dolce

On Murray's Run

Poems & Lyrics

Selected by Les Murray

Special Thanks

Suzanne Edgar, Dan Guenther, Alan Gould, Geoff Page,
Robbie Coburn, Houston Dunleavy, Michael Warren Davis,
George Thomas, Mark Tredinnick, Philip Nitschke,
Stephen Matthews and Matthew von Baeyer.

On Murray's Run: Poems & Lyrics
ISBN 978 1 76041 419 1
Copyright © text Joe Dolce 2017
Cover from a painting by Lin van Hek

First published 2017 by
GINNINDERRA PRESS
PO Box 3461 Port Adelaide 5015 Australia
www.ginninderrapress.com.au

Contents

Foreword	11
Preface	13
Poems	19
Inzuppare Il Biscotto	21
A Kid'll Eat Ivy Too	22
J Effen K	23
Overextended Family	26
The Hustler	27
Elegy For Old Feller	28
Kinetoscope Beating	29
Pin Boy	30
Little Grandpa Train Ride	33
The Fading Art of Write	35
Daybirth	36
The Gas That Killed Sylvia Plath	37
The Poetess	38
How Many Poets Does It Change To Take a Light Bulb?	41
The Kissing Disease	42
Conjuring Phó	43
Thịt Chó	44
The Red Napoleon	45
Camelus	46
Flu Fanculo	47
Sketch	48
St Josephine	49
My Soul To Keep	50
Joseph Jack and Mary Jill	51
A Few Words On the Birthday of Barry St Vitus	52
Gruß Vom Krampus	53
Scatomancy	54

Souls	55
Pullus Cosmologica	56
The Big C Word	58
The Left	60
The Right	62
An Inconvenient Frogsicle	63
Whoso Curseth	64
A Worm's Point of View On Clichés	66
Bedbug Dreaming	67
Birthday	68
Imaginary Gardens Real Toads	70
Kite	72
Lost Haiku of Osama Bin Laden	73
Rude At 4 a.m.	74
The Dr. Seuss That Switched His Voice	75
A Loon Sang In Walloon	77
This Town Ain't Big Enough For Two Giuseppes	78
Ulysses For Italians	80
Lemonscent	81
A Shoe Is a Shoe Is a Shoe	82
Last-minute Gift Ideas For the Cheating Ex-	84
In the Manner of Cavafy	85
Jolokia	86
Masturbari	87
Distant Relations	89
Music 101	90
Robin Hood Roulette	91
Shuffleboard	92
Thirty-three Years of Bliss	94
Apparition	95
Short Wave	96
The Daughter That Still Loves Me	97

Arl	98
Ode Al Dente	100
If Hitler Also Spelled Hiedler	102
Blondi	103
Can You Write Left-Handed Poetry?	104
Kilroy	105
War and Peace Senryu	107
The Jimmy Leg	108
Reconciliation Haiku	109
Petrolhead Zen	110
Lorca Said I Can Conceive	111
Letter From the King	112
If Good News Sold Newspapers	113
I Set a Mousetrap Late Last Night	114
The Rime of the Ancient Gooney Bird	115
Chicago Typewriter	116
Chess Player	117
Skeptic's Friday	118
Spock	119
Leechcraft	120
Tick	121
Agony Aunts	122
Nachtmahr	124
Noh Means Noh	125
Breakaleg	126
A Charming Bath	127
Ice Ann	129
Bonyi	132
Sandmen	133
Pokie Poem	135
Evil Eye	136
Natte Yallock Jump Rope	137

Where Is the Poetry In Pain?	138
Voltaire Left	139
The Days of Real Door-to-door Are Done	140
Tucker's Caravan	141
Blackman With Dementia	143
Da Vinci Was a Bastard	145
Three-ring Fleas	146
Green Dream	147
Ag	148
Chewy Blues	149
Close Encounters of the Blowfly Kind	150
Possomnia	151
Cullinan	152
Poetry Is Like Looking	153
A Rune of One's Own	154
Ode To a Bush Dunny	155
Toothsome	156
Sense of Out-of-place	158
I Dreamt I Saw St Augustine (St Dominic As Well)	160
An Interesting Little Girl	162
Little Blue Book	163

Lyrics 165

The Green-eyed Boy of the Rain	167
The Ballad of the Gangster Paul Kelly	168
Transportation To America	170
Black Caesar: the First Bushranger	171
Harry Power: the Last Bushranger	172
Dry Whisky Tongue	175
Mr Critical	176
Mr Q	177
Out of Book	179
The Awful Flanders and Wallonia Train Wreck	180

Dead Cat Bounce	181
Everything Is Fixed	183
I Never Found Those Lips Again	184
Jean La Pucelle	185
Lullaby Redux	187
In the Next Life	188
from The Leadbelly Ballad Novel	189
Jack Johnson and the Mann Act	191
Give Me Little Sugar With My Beer Sylvie	193
Marie Laveau La Belle Voodooienne	194
The Happiest Times I Ever Had…	196
Jelly With My Cake Blues	199
Lead	200
Pig Tails In Gravy	202
Red Velvet Cake	203
Houston Riot of 1917	204
Eli Whitney and the Cotton Gin	205
Lafayette's Mixture	207
Gideon Bible	208
Orpheo Don't Look Back	209
About the author	210

Foreword

Renowned songwriter Joe Dolce has long outgrown the pop lyric and moved into a risky domain where recitative, comedy, folk and slapstick build shelters for themselves among social commentary and the poetry of lists. He has a foot, or feet, in diverse realms serious and entertaining and has resolved that he will never record another song that has not been first published as a stand-alone poem. No colleague to his knowledge has yet ventured into this territory yet its potentials for escape from the shiftily High Serious and the narrow criteria of academic critique are obvious. Wit, and the songwriter's freedoms of seeing one's creations recorded by others, are possible bases for a jazz-like shift in the profession of poetry, and music remains available to float logjams that commentary is apt to desiccate. Since coming to *Quadrant* as a regular contributor, he has built a real following for his work, and we'll miss him when his vogue spreads beyond our pages.

Les Murray

Preface

When writing about this collection of poems, I am aware of the long tradition of critical response from the inner sanctum of a poet's life. These early responses to the work can be savage reminders to the poet that someone is listening very closely and with none of the distance of the wider audience that may or may not become the readers.

When Emily Dickinson wrote 'My life had stood – a Loaded Gun', it was to her sister-in-law, Susan Gilbert, who lived next door, and who knew the reckless turmoil that existed in that towering citadel of nervy sexual restraint engulfing those two adjoined households in rural Amherst. The wife of her adulterous brother, Austin, had a complex love relationship for thirty-five years with the poet and was the first reader of the work that the poet called blossoms of the mind. Decades of scholarship have revealed her work as being anything but this over-sentimentalised description. This monumental confrontation of the greatest poetic potency, a synthesis of penetrating erotic yearning and enforced passivity: the wind is like 'hungry dogs', her dark visions and contemptuous witticisms are often reserved 'for the son who came to justify the ways of God to man'. Her cynical surrealism and anti-religious stance is unparalleled among great poets and far from the blossoms of the mind to which she inscribed her offerings.

Ted Hughes was the first to write admiringly about his wife Sylvia Plath's artisan approach to her work. Leaving no work unfinished, she persisted until a completed verse had been achieved. 'If she could not get a table out of the material, she was happy with a chair, or even a toy.'

The congenial companionship of Wordsworth and sister Dorothy, roaming the pastoral landscape for inspiration:

'Listen, Dorothy: I wandered lonely as a cow…'

'Perhaps, dear, you may like to try "cloud".'

'Yes,' he replied, 'that's it! I wandered lonely as a cloud!'

When Vita Sackville West called Virginia Woolf a genius, in public, she was admonished by her friend, 'Oh God, don't say that – no one will ever believe a word I say again.'

Dylan Thomas returned from yet another tremendously successful tour of America, with no money in his pocket, confirming his wife Caitlin's belief that his scribbling was total crap and did not feed their children. At home, in Wales, Thomas wrote in the boathouse, in between his drinking, and spent all the money he made from touring by shouting free drinks to everyone in the bars. Caitlin regularly heard his poems, read aloud in the bath, but could only ask, 'And how much would that one be worth?'

But Dylan Thomas's performances in America were the nearest that any poet came to a rock concert status. He was feted and adored everywhere he went and provided with drugs and alcohol that would take him to an early grave.

T.S. Eliot took to his sickbed during the writing of *The Waste Land*, and his wife, Vivienne Haigh-Wood, took up the running of his affairs, including the finishing of the poem. She wrote forty lines, which he later claimed were the best in 'the whole bloody thing'. Of course, after a while, the marriage went bad and he joined forces with her brother to have her committed to a mental asylum, where she spent the rest of her life. Though the forty lines remained, no one mentioned her name again.

At times, I have listened to Joe's raw verse in the breakfast hour and admired his ingenuity. I have been there for the metaphors that spring up around life's flotsam, births, deaths, marriages and hair loss. This is not a Protestant Wordsworth, or a pagan Coleridge, but a man of stupefying energy, with a combative spirit, not a man likely to stand down.

When a poet makes contact, it can be like a tick bite on one's vitals, or a funeral procession of thoughts and a distancing of self and world. It can also be a cinematic mirage surrounding you with a vapour of entrancement.

Do not expect a slim elegant volume with each poem melting into the last. Nor is it a work of modest scope. Conceptually vast, he sometimes takes his imagery from the domestic arts, the disclosures of daily custom, like the shopper picking through tomatoes at the market. Always there is the awareness of the relation of form and content. His mind is a calm well-ordered desk; he delivers his American experience with a sharpened pencil in the 'J Effen K' poem, continuing the riff of Ferlingetti's 'I'm waiting for them to prove that God is really an American'.

In the What if poems, what if Sylvia had actually killed Ted? Bequeathing the Poetess three grandchildren, turning the scandal on its head.

In 'If Hitler Also Spelled Hiedler', what if Hitler had actually been accepted to the Academy of Fine Arts, Vienna?

The beautiful 'Green-eyed Boy of the Rain' – almost a murder ballad, the destruction of a human objet d'art:

> I wanted to kill him to tear him apart,
> Until nothing of him would remain,
> When I thought of him kissing her mouth,
> The green-eyed boy of the rain.

At twenty-three, he came into the orbit of a gifted literary mentor, in Montreal, Canada – Matthew von Baeyer. Von Baeyer taught English at McGill University and was legendary in those parts for his love and knowledge of poetry. One of his short inscriptions to Dolce sums up his unique teaching philosophy: 'All REAL teaching is done personally, deeply – and mutually'.

Von Baeyer also happened to be a brilliant live poetry reader, with an evocative voice and timing that rendered poems impossible to ignore. He asked the young Dolce to compose music for the poetry, requesting he accompany him at readings. It was in this manner that some of the greatest poetic works ever written, repeatedly heard and performed, became ingrained in his sensibilities. The apprenticeship, of sorts, stayed with him and though he later immersed himself in the musical opportunities of the 1970s, this early literary experience remained as a heady romantic overture to his life. One of his first recordings, in 1980, was 'Return', a poem by Greek poet, C.P. Cavafy, that he had set to music, in 1969:

> Return often and take me beloved sensation,
> return and take me,
> when the lips and the skin remember.

There would be many detours before Dolce returned to where he started. Like an old man who marries his childhood sweetheart, he has taken up where he left off with determined passions ramming against each other. This volume is not a record of all the poems and song lyrics written in the last seven years, but rather the ones chosen by the poet extraordinaire, and literary editor, Les Murray. More than 150, to date.

There are many to choose from, coming comet-like,

sometimes with the dangerous radiance of art kept under quarantine. The volume teems with personalities: Mr Q – the hometown paedophile. Bushranger Harry Power. Albert Tucker building his caravan from a bedsit in Paris.

His palette drifts into psychedelic amber with 'The Big C Word' and 'Da Vinci Was a Bastard'. The balefully grave understudy to a love poem, 'Apparition', stands alone, naked. A small transfusion of untamed fear if you believe that our life is reshaped in our art.

There's that cinematic time capsule standing whole and intact, 'Little Grandpa Train Ride', an entire immigrant story captured on one page. Great-grandfather cut in two by the silent steam train, the small grandson taken on board for a ride on the choo choo, carried home in sooty arms, scarred cap hung on the kitchen hook, the older man finally sitting, demented, in the garden, while grandchildren knock his cap off and play choo choo, themselves, all about him.

In fact, this same deep well of recollection served him amply when he wrote,

> When I was a boy
> about the eighth grade
> mama used to say
> don't stay out late
> with the bad boys
> always shoot-a pool…

It was this simple verse set to music, selling on vinyl, in fifteen countries, translated into as many languages, never masquerading as poetry, merely testimony, understood across the world, no barriers of language, instantly recognisable by his peoples, the unsettled, the relocated. The women, with nothing but a small suitcase holding their wedding sheets, called wogs, and niggers, for a few decades, before uneasy acceptance. Above all, the fathers and sons accepting shit work, while living ten to a room, until they saved enough money to send for wives and mothers to join them in this 'a nice-a place'.

If you have any doubt that this book could be a fascinating read, then consider the coupling: this country's most important poet, untethered by the boundaries of country, culture or language; and the other, the composer, today seventy years old, who has himself wandered the corridors of international popularity.

There were many knock-backs; self-enquiry that said, is that all you can summon up from the dark heart of existence?

Then, occasionally, editorial encouragement to lift the spirit.

As Murray once told him, 'When you do it well, you are Zowie!'

Lin van Hek, Carlton, Victoria, 2017

Poems

Inzuppare Il Biscotto

(Italian: 'to soak the biscuit' – that is, to have sex)

Who could resist
that Butternut Snap lap
crumbly like an
Anzac in the sack
Scotch Finger steady
on the Tiny Teddy
Swallow's Bush Biscuit
Milk Arrowroot and
Adora Cream lips breathlessly
mumblin' the
Honey Jumble?

A Kid'll Eat Ivy Too

we were Dolce pronounced doltz

to blend in
better with non-Italians in our small Ohio town

mares eat oats and does eat doltz and little lambs eat ivy
classmates used to tease
but at college I became dolcháy

precisely in order

to blend out

infrequent time travel trips to visit family
devolve me occasionally back into doltz
for wrinkle-free camouflage

J Effen K

Time upon a once
an ago time along
when America was so grand-
stand free of the home-
less and a brave land

and reporters exploded flashguns
before school guns flashed,
when priests were lit with God
and Superman said please
and politicians held little Johnnies
and doctors killed disease,

a boy was a once
sat at a school desk gazing
and the principal's voice
like a loud god amazing
on the class intercom
could stop Chemistry.

When TVs looked like fishbowls
and mom ironed shirts,
sewed holes
and cooked dinners
secretaries ran the switchboard poles
and dad shovelled snow in winters

before doctors were in newspapers
and priests touched little Johnnies
there above the knees
and politicians talked to God
and reporters spread contagious disease,

a boy was a once
in a far land aways
ever happily after
catching a ball
once
(before replays)
and journalists cried
when dreams died.

Before Marilyns were breathless –
gangsters were just Cagney
or Edward G
and Oswald was a flying owl
and Superman flew on TV,

before television was a fishbowl
and dad fucked the secretaries
(he had to work late, see?)
and mom stopped eating
and snow buried memories,

a boy was a once,
fell asleep at a book,
flew out of the schoolroom,
hit the ground, bounced,
scraping a knee,
and up for better look,
got caught in a tree.

When doctors gave shots
for scrapes
and measles and mumps
and out of a window
Superman jumped
but could no longer fly,
before Clark Kent died,

before Elvis was shot,
needles
played records,
before Sinatra got fat
and mom and dad fought
and sparrows sang flat

and journalists wrote
like birds
and men

like Walter Cronkite cried
when he heard
J Effen K had died.

Overextended Family

My uncle was a gambler
he opened the boot of his new '57 Ford
showed ten-year-old me the green suitcase
of one hundred new decks
of playing cards seals unbroken

his daughter my first cousin married
someone crazy no-good
one day after a domestic
he unloaded his shotgun through
the trailer door killing her

his oldest son drunk
and mouthing off at a family lunch
was decked by my eighty-year-old father
who knocked him out with one punch.

The Hustler

Manny's Pool Hall Cleveland 1962
Kirk had the driver's licence the four of us
high school boys owned brass-jointed cues
to break in half and fold into a leather pouch
carry-strap young gunslingers
emulating Fast Eddie and Minnesota Fats
from Walter Tevis' book and film
although I was never completely convinced
about comedian Jackie Gleason as Fats (until much later)
always seeing Ralph Kramden, his one of these days, Alice…
to the MOON! from *The Honeymooners*
what really scared me was Paul Newman
thumbs broken in the cheap toilet stall

Kirk was my age and the first authentic hustler
I ever knew he was gifted
when any of us played for fun
he always lost praising our skill
dismissing his own month after month
when Kirk played for money against strangers or us
he invariably won apologising for his luck
returning to casual free play
his losing streak returned
the sincerity with which Kirk convinced me
putting his arm around my shoulder
actually made me feel good about myself
my own ability I observed this exact behaviour
years later in friends of mine
who were junkies.

Elegy For Old Feller

The little old bloke nose like a tomato
from too much grog has vanished
scrawny in his slept-in clothes
he walked an even scrawnier dog
past our house for years
muttering at the unseen
I never spoke to him except once
to invite him to a neighbourly block
barbecue out on the nature strip
come over and have a sausage I said
naw I don't eat foreign food.

Kinetoscope Beating

My father hitting small child of me split
selves one cat-jumping upwards to safety
looking down the other crushed to kitchen floor
staring up at a giant wearing Death
five senses five sponges soak up
cold linoleum against cheek the bloom
of my mother's red mouth mute
her Maidenform whispering through blue angora
her eyes fear teary
I taste salt and dusty floor detergent
inhaling kitchen fragrances & Old Spice
the Marx Brothers shout from front room tv
my own screaming fetus position
folding inward an anemone
his coarse skinned hand
reverberating off my body

the two camera positions of split selves
splice perspective cuts
accelerating shuddering oscillations
as we shake together again into one child
my anxious mother bending over me
I see him flickering through the doorway
like some great ghost animal vanishing into the blind
and I am in focus again.

Pin Boy

The bowling pins were ducks
wooden decoys heavy in the hand
weighted statuettes in plastic jackets
polished and white with red neck stripes
dented here and here where they had slammed
against other pins in endless spares and strikes

my summer job was loading
a pin carriage with the ten men lowering it
onto the alley with a lever before automation
the pinboy got two dollars an hour

my father managed the bowling alley
the best he could get in a sport
he once was passionate and skilled at
before he put his ball in the leather bag
in the front closet forever

he was local-famous for a couple of years
a champ in the US Army
in the early sixties I watched him bowl
other bowling men in monogrammed silk shirts
my mother brought me to the tournaments
we'd sit behind a rail
I watched him do his distinctive trot
down the lane releasing the ball arcing impossibly
into the pin pocket strike after strike
to sustain his 270 average although
he never achieved the holy grail 300 game
twelve strikes in a row

I liked looking at him
on the TV monitor above
the scoring station where the man wrote Xs
and diagonal strokes on odd rectangular paper
filling small boxes after each toss

watching my father on the screen
felt important one year he had a run
we thought he could never lose but he lost
and the TV show was over

he took a job managing the bowling alley
trading on local renown until even that
was a dim memory later turning to carpentry
building the first malls and his own house

for the pension he went back
to his pre-war job at the post office
where he woke every morning at 4 a.m.
until he died

my father never bowled again even for pleasure
the worn ball stayed in the front closet
motionless in its two-toned zippered bag

once I asked him why he stopped
he never could verbalise it but it seemed
like it was a painful thing for him to consider

years later after the funeral
I cleaned out his condo closets
I never found that old ball
he must have eventually thrown it out
along with his shotguns twelve gauge shells
and the inscrutable wooden ducks.

Little Grandpa Train Ride

Not quite Casey Jones
my little grandpa (to distinguish
from grandma's father big grandpa)
early engineered the Baltimore & Ohio
steam engines passing behind our Painesville house
he often took me on rides sat me
in the high steel seat near him
the Iron Horse throwing
a ribbony white steam scarf behind
I gazed at vibrating dials handles
wooden water towers landscapes whizzing to sides
as he reached into stacked woodpile
behind open cab feeding the eating red furnace
choo chooing me through childhood
ride over carried home in sooty arms
he always hanged his striped railroad cap
on a hook at the back screen door
later retired from tracks continuing
at the new Diamond Alkalai
synthetic rayon plant until
toxic smoke took his lungs
he sat in the windowed veranda
of the old Owego Street house filling
brown pipes mostly silent
until a buzzing grandkid would ask
about railroads the correct password
he talked repetitively of a single memory
of his own hard-of-hearing engineer father
cut in half by a silent engine
lantern-walking the centre of a railyard track

officials woke his mother at three a.m.
to take her out to the cut body
my little grandpa hearing
everything from beneath his cover
this worn story coupled directly

to the great skipping-record nightmare
he was plagued with for years until he died
the big nigger with the axe, Joey
as he said chasing him down the night
after senility had severed
his mind little grandpa sat in his neglected garden
small kids flitting around him
like landscapes little laughing hands like wind
knocking off the long-faded striped cap
sitting in wonder in his seat watching
with smoky eyes his great-grandchildren
now choo chooing him off.

The Fading Art of Write

Letters typewrite onto the page
crisp little taps standing at attention
identical height width length
in latest designer font
dressed by Garamond and Caslon
while actual handwriting
eaten by moths is left
in tie-bags outside St Vinnies

endless childhood hours spent
drawing perfect letters on ruled paper
keeping Os Rs and Ws neatly
framed between parallel lines
have come to naught

I long for the script and whorl
of home-made handwriting again
my granddaughter a Benedictine monk
sits patiently at kitchen table
slowly crafting single letters

I will steal some of her blue-striped paper
and try to earn the gold star.

Daybirth

for Lin van Hek

Lin née Whitehead fair-headed of all
a mirrorpool at foot of the waterfall
these the Old English bard might call
fine flax or flowering Linden tree
the drunken Scot staggering see
or Eibhleann when French uprooted to Éirinn
by Norman invaders settling therein
the pleasant and beautiful radiant fair Lin
the steepest ravine the precipice
the black pool as in Dublin
some Gaels would insist
but all entwined fire
there by her love lit
breithlá sona duit.*

* Irish-Gaelic for Happy Birthday.
Pronunciations:
breithlá sona duit (BREH-huh SON-uh gwit)
Eibhleann (AVE-linn)
Éirinn (AYR-ihn)
Gaels (gales)

The Gas That Killed Sylvia Plath

The gas that killed Sylvia Plath
didn't rise as she hoped lighter than air
but heavier sank to the floor through cracks
penetrating the lower flats there

the gas that killed Sylvia Plath
left Mr Thomas comatose below
neither understanding her grief nor sharing her wrath
he slept breathing in the tranquil flow

the gas that killed Sylvia Plath
turned her blood bright pink and thin
tilted her mind down death's slanting path
leaving a residuum of cherry-red skin.

The Poetess

The door wet-towelled
from inside to prevent leakage
required a workman's shoulder
despite a key fighting off
carbon monoxide gag
windows quickly prised open
discovering the kneeling body in repose
the poet's head thrust far
into the old Rangemaster oven
no explanatory note

where are the two children…

through the imagined breathing window
geese fly in reverse
night gives way to sunset
and hands counter-clock
in the temporal shift of what if…

the poetess is arrested pusher-walking
two infants blocks away
a confessional diary held tightly
reveals his abuse her plan unfaithful
husband invited to tea to talk
drugged drink better him than her she thought

the poetess in our alternate
judged guilty of murder
a life sentence continues writing
incarcerated recognition
in certain circles is declared a new Genet

the dead husband's pregnant mistress bears
an illegitimate daughter remarrying
an understanding man quietly in Israel
the child grows up beautiful and good

the son of the poetess at fifteen begins prison visits
assuming the role of mother's protector
a passion for wildlife encouraged by her love
leads to his own mystical nature poetry
marriage to an Australian photographer
retreat to the Hawkesbury River
bequeathing the poetess three grandchildren

the daughter of the poetess eighteen
adamantly refusing to have anything to do with the mother
dutifully champions her late father's unrealised work

the poetess over time attracts international recognition
first in the US later the UK
public support and petition force her
early release after only fifteen served
cult movement supporters of murdered husband
outraged at leniency stage protests at literary festivals

the poetess at forty-six relocates back to US
retaining close acquaintance with newly minted
British Laureate Larkin who attributes her inspiration
to overcoming the writer's block originally preventing
his acceptance of the award

the poetess sustains two further long-term affairs
one with a woman she never remarries
releasing her final volume
The Funeral Postcards
in the year of her passing at eighty-five the poems absolute
and honest contrition
for the murder of her husband astound
the literary world
winning the Pulitzer Prize
after death the unburnt diary seized
at the time of arrest is canonised
beside the confessional notebooks
of Countess Tolstoy and Cosima Wagner

the longtime estranged daughter of the poetess
at fifty-three a successful art critic
marries a man three years junior
a man in black with a Mein Kampf look

a year later she forgives
the poetess her mother
for the death of her father.

How Many Poets Does It Change To Take a Light Bulb?

I Sing the Light Bulb Electric
once a jolly light globe
burnt out over Billy's bong
a light bulb is a light bulb is a light bulb

light globes to the right of me
light globes to the left of me
bursting and blackened

the force that through the green globe no longer lights the dunny
does not go gentle into that dark night
and you my father on that stepladder height
change change the dying of the light
I was just ten when they tried to change you
that black bulb that blew my pretty red heart in two
will you change it change it change it?
There was movement at the socket
for the bulb was passed around
when the filament from The Previous had burnt away
begging that bulb between our teeth to light
keep going brighten spark … but set us free
and then we saw the wild boys of the hallway
with fresh bulbs in their hands
go running after it
five bulbs the bumpkin calculus of Light
your echoes die your voice is dowsed by Dark
there's not a Pygmy can reach the ceiling

and light bulbs to change before I sleep
and light bulbs to change before…*zzzzzzzzzzz*

The Kissing Disease

Where HIV virus can be retro and lethal
and said to be spread by monkey and needle
from drink bottle sharing & lips mono jumps
kissin' cousin of herpes and chickenpox bumps
pillows toothbrushes cups cigarettes
forks straws saliva begets
glandular fever mononucleosis
attributed to (EBV) Epstein-Barr virus
tonsils become inflamed ache in the liver
sore throat fever night sweats shiver
bane of schooldays swollen lymph glands
the most reliable home cure: just washing your hands
gargling salt water to ease a sore throat
paracetamol and bowls of chicken soup – take note
bed rest a quarantine sign on the door
no kissing or canoodling for three months more.

Conjuring Phó

Boiled clean beef ribs
pile-stacked like
xylophone wood

industrial-sized *pot-au-feu*
balancing on point
single pre-Indochina War gas jet
bubbling brown bath at first glance
more dishwater-dressed than stock

miraculously grandmother transformed
into a bowl of richest broth
sea dragon cellophane rice noodles
verdant flecked chives white baby
spring onion sliced red chili squeezed
lime fragrant star anise

Hanoi street alchemy
priceless at two dollars.

Thịt Chó

Removing shoes
in deference to some local deity
or muddy track
barefoot onto worn tatami mat
we sit cross-legged at newspaper
covered low tables

the irony of the next-door pet
hospital's proximity to the restaurant is not lost

a tray arrives with rau ram leaves
piled on plates small saucers
of salt hilled in lime juice
cold bottles of Bia Ha Noi

the anticipated main is served
and thankfully does not taste like chicken
but delicious dark smoked uncrackled pork

later after helmetless monkey-hug
motorbike ride along the Song Hong
through Bladerunner streets
skydiving at ground level
you ask me what the meal was like
I reply that if you threw a stick
and yelled fetch
you'd be waiting a long time.

The Red Napoleon

or his own preferred name for himself
General of Peace Võ Nguyên Giáp
the grand brother of Uncle Ho's army
led Vietminh guerillas
against Japanese invaders during World War II
against French against Americans
compared to Cyrus the Great
Chandragupta of India studied Mao
applied lessons to anti-colonialist struggle
communism grafted onto a national rootstock
educated in law taught history worked as a journalist
enjoyed Goethe Shakespeare Tolstoy
some popular quotes:

the enemy does not possess the psychological
and physical means to fight a long drawn out war

father arrested by French and died in prison
wife arrested by French and died in prison
remarried – five children

Americans think, pawns of government
Vietnamese think, united with government

General Giáp had a fiery temper a dandy
dressed in white suit vs Ho car-tyre sandals & shorts
was criticised repeatedly for excessive verbosity of writing style
no formal military training he joked
I attended the academy of the bush

invented the Ho Chi Minh trail
died October 4th 2013
102 years of age.

Camelus

'A camel makes an elephant feel like a jet plane.' – Jackie Kennedy

Males have a dulla in neck
inflatable sac extruding from mouth
resembling a swollen tongue when in rut
to attract females red blood
cells are oval not round
faeces dry enough to fuel fires
gait wide even-toed feet stop sinking in sand
descended from the same rabbit-sized
ancestor as pigs Native Americans wiped out
wild ones before adopting buffalo
Etruscan saddles first appeared on humps in 1200 BC
Roman legions used combat dromedarii to scare off horses
Heliogabalus and Cleopatra ate the heel
tough meat best slow-cooked and roasted whole
halal for muslim not-kosher for jews
milk is medicine and aphrodisiac
urine a thick syrup Mohammed
ordered people to drink it for health
the Abu Dhabi Officer's Club serves burgers
camel lasagne can be eaten in Alice Springs curry in Sydney
the feral population of Central Australia
presently one million growing at 8% a year
a cama is a hybrid of the camel and llama
inheriting the poor temperament of both.

Flu Fanculo

Horror coaster cough roaring
out Luna Park lungs razor shearing
throat tunnel and tracks sinus implosion
spraying a two-foot perimeter explosion
as close to an epileptic twist as you get
without having a jacked-up Jerry Lewis fit
empty tissue boxes rising like M15 mags
wastebasket brimming wet burning metal rags
how many different hacking sounds can a throat make?
I scare myself to sleep I scare others awake
stomach acid mixed in with thick gluey glug
hell throat contracting around stuck plug
always waiting for the Big Red Clot
the tissue of blood the TB flag the passing out
on bathroom floor the bloodshot eye soup
but so far just yellow goop

oh there is an infection no doubt
viral or bacterial
it's immaterial
I regress straight back to a childhood bout

of survivor mentality the colds the clinging
the shots the sore arm the Bay Leaf tea mama's bringing
the medicinal mend
glorious school wag excusable
was mich nicht umbringt macht mich elend
what doesn't kill me makes me miserable.

Sketch

The sketch was done when
we were both much younger
friends commented on the uncanny
accuracy I achieved his eyes clear and
ready to receive Light his hair
curled and soft on his neck before
it became marred with blood
lips moist full and ripe
to speak the Word he would soon be given

now I am old and they bless
my old friend as The Last Prophet
it is no longer possible by Law
to depict him in any way

still I have this early sketch
friends said it was an accurate likeness
I can never show it to anyone now
Followers would destroy both it and me
what shall become of it?

I will roll it carefully
wrap it in tiraz cloth
appeal to the King of Cockroaches
O Kabi:kaj do not eat this paper
and seal it in a sturdy Meccan urn

perhaps one day after I have entered Paradise
someone will find it
in a more generous time
when it is no longer forbidden
to gaze upon His image.

St Josephine

Josephine Margaret Bakhita
kidnapped by slave traders
torn from family in Darfur and robbed
of childhood at seven
sold resold five times
in markets of El Obeid and Khartoum
named Bakhita by captors – Arabic for lucky –
(she eventually forgot her birth name).
Scarified and tattooed with razor, salt, white flour,
114 patterns cut into breasts, belly and arms.
Forcibly converted to Islam.

Bought by an Italian Consul, a kind man.
Brought to Italy and Christ,
entrusted to the Canossian Sisters,
trained in the catechumenate in Venice,
received communion from Cardinal Sarto,
the future Pope Pius X.

Her mind on God, her heart in Africa,
she was known as *madre moretta*, black mother.
She named God the Master,
while dying whispered,
please loosen these chains…they are heavy,
her final words – Our lady! Our lady!

Canonised by Pope John Paul II,
the only Sudanese saint,
patron of evangelical reconciliation.

My Soul To Keep

Now I lay me down to sleep
eight hours of every night I slip
into unconsciousness and skip
one third of every day I keep

in darkness counting secret sheep
a third of life is lost
to dreaming turned and dreamless tossed
I pray the Lord my soul to keep

my sixty-year-old bones are bare
forty in the light the other
twenty spent beneath a cover
oblivious it's hardly fair

if I could ration down to four
those hours each night I forsake
if I should die before I wake
four extra hours would give more

life awake and love to ache
of course the dreaming time be less
perhaps the way it is is best
I pray the Lord my soul to take.

Joseph Jack and Mary Jill

Joseph Jack and Mary Jill
goeth up Golgotha Hill
to fetch a pail
of blood and nail.

A Few Words On the Birthday of Barry St Vitus

On your birthday St Vitus no weeping
all the dancers and actors will be leaping
for you without taint
are the great patron saint
of lightning-strike jokes & late sleeping.

Gruß Vom Krampus

Then let us go and be terrible.

He's making his list,
and you're on it twice,
punishes children,
naughty and nice.
Krampus is coming to town.

He's horned and heathen,
a long pointed tongue,
with burnt-out candles,
his wagon is strung.
Krampus is coming to town.

Washtub on his back,
a beard full of bats,
he carries in his claws,
a birch to swat brats.
Krampus is coming to town.

With sacks full of coal,
a clanging of bells,
he empties his bags,
to haul kids to Hell.
Krampus is coming to town.

He'll steal the Julbocken,
the Childermas goat,
come disguised as candy,
until it's stuck in your throat.
Krampus, the Christmas devil, is coming to town

Scatomancy

Divination by excrement,
it goes way back,
Egyptians had dung beetles
to forebode the track.

Séance *dans la toilette*
might draw quite a queue,
spirit voices in flatulence:
Uncle John, is that you?

Levitating the seat,
with knocks and a spasm,
(but don't get me started
on ectoplasm.)

Add some Tassology,
a discount price tag,
you fast and drink tea,
then eat the tea bag.

The Age might be keen
on a regular forecast,
or, apropos,
a daily aftcast.

My column would be practical,
The Phoenix, fourth page,
after auguring the omen,
you could line the birdcage.

Souls

Some words form souls
of other words.

In Hawaiian,
Ua – rain– is soul of
Hua – fruit,
Pua – flower.

Ua sounds
the way rain feels,

ooooahhh

Rain falls in Kaua – us,
and Aloha Kaua –
may there be love
between us.

Pullus Cosmologica

'Which came first– the chicken or the road?' – Anon Chook

Shakespeare Chook:
To cross or not to cross
THAT is the question…

Frost Chook:
Two roads diverged in a wood, and I
I crossed the one less crossed by,
And that has made all the difference

Descartes Chook:
I cross, therefore I am

Poe Chook:
On this road by horror haunted
Tell me truly I implore
Crossed the Chicken never more.

Kerouac Chook Book:
Cross the Road

Whitman Chook:
Afoot and light-hearted I cross the open road
Henceforth I ask not good-fortune,
I myself am good-fortune,
Henceforth I cluck no more…

Plath Chook:
You do not do you do not do
anymore black road over which have I cock-a-doodled do…

Lawson Chook:
But not until a city feels red rooster's feet
Shall its sad people miss awhile the terrors of the street
The dreadful everlasting stride scarcely feathers and meat…

Emerson Chook:
Do not cross at the crossing rail,
cross instead where there is no road and leave a trail.

Teddy Roosevelt Chook:
Cross softly and carry a big beak.

JFK Chook:
So ask not what your road can do for you,
Ask what you can do for your road.

Clinton Chook:
I did not have sex with that road.

Whitlam Chook:
Ladies and gentlemen, well may we say 'God cross the Road'…

The Big C Word

The big C word sounds loud on trams
the big C word scares lemmings and lambs
the big C word gets attention in banks
the big C word in China stops tanks

it's hard to argue with The big C word
the big C word will always be heard

they've tried to kill it with pills and gas
they've tried to quiet it with confession and Mass
they're tried to silence it in hospitals and class
they've tried to show it behinds bars and glass
they've tried to kick it in the teeth and the ass

the big C word always gets up
the big C word just wont shut up

the big C word can halt conversation
the big C word doesn't need invitation
the big C word will get you people's sympathy
the C word is big like a people's symphony
the C word is louder than a Kalashnikov gun
the C word will burn you like a Red Giant Sun
the C word is more invasive than the Hun
the C word can crack the unbreakable locks
the C word will put you in a six-sided box
the big C word survived Berlin & Vietnam
it can eat up your skin like an atom bomb
it can tattoo your arm like a Holocaust victim
& make you skinny like Twiggys or how fashion depicts 'em

it's hard to argue with the big C word
the big C word will always be heard

the big C word can lower down the rich
the big C word gives politicians a stitch
the big C word is the raw red Itch
the big C word is the Bona Fide Bitch
you just can't teach it with prayers or law
you can't cut it out with a knife or a saw

can't spray it away with insecticide or pepper
you can't exile it to an island like a Leper

the big C word will always be heard
the big C word always has the last word.

The Left

Barack Obama is Left
so is George H.W. Bush

10% of the world is Left
first identified in a fetus
by the hand held closest to the mouth
Sign of the Devil from sinistrality sinister
Latin *sinus* meaning pocket Roman togas
having only one on the Left side
German *linkshänder* French *gauche* clumsy graceless awkward
Dutch *twee linkerhanden hebben* is to have two Left hands
in Hebrew Left symbolised power to shame society
brought to Christianity as Natural Evil by Ambrose of Milan
in Ghana to sleep on the Left side is to be dead
an insult to shake with the Left
but encouraged as in India for chamber pots and excreta
southpaw goofy cack-handed from Latin *cacare*
downunder a Molly-Duker
not always negative
Roman *augures* proceeded from the East
the Russian *levsha* a skilled craftsman
in Leskov's 'Tale of the Cross-eyed Lefty'
items somewhat inconvenient for the Left:
cameras can openers fishing reels
on-off switches on dangerous machinery
firearms chequebooks boomerangs
the QWERTY keyboard favours Left
3,000 English words typed with only the Left
compared to 300 with the Right

the Left earns 10–15% more than the Right
statisticians say Left is increasing

Clinton is Left
so was Reagan.

The Right

George W. Bush was Right,
so was Jimmy Carter.

90% of the world is Right.
Right reaches puberty five months earlier than Left.
Latin *dextera Domini* – sitting on the Right of God.
German *rechtshänder*, French *droit* – direct, straight, Law.
Most scripts read Left to Right.
Dutch *Laat uw linkerhand niet weten wat uw rechterhand doet* –
let your Left know what your Right is doing.
Chinese Muslims eat only with the Right –
in a typical household, the wife sits to the Right,
in bed, she lay on the Left.
In Taiwan, Left are strongly encouraged to switch to Right –
but stuttering and dyslexia often happen, if forced Right.
Rats and monkeys favour the Right for handling things.
The Right tend toward rational, analytic; the Left holistic.
Left generally zigzag, bump noses, when kissing Right.
In machinery, the Right twists clockwise, receding from the observer.
Standard playing cards fan to the Right for visible numbers.
The Right differs from the Left by one IQ point.
The Right live nine years longer than the Left.
Statisticians say Right is decreasing

Richard Nixon was Right,
so was JFK.

An Inconvenient Frogsicle

Real frogs behave differently. Paul Krugman

Toss them in 100°C water – they frog-leap out.
But gradually increase heat,
at rate less than .2°C per minute,
and dull-witted amphibians dreamily
croak off to Elysium lily pads –

or so the story goes, according to Sedgwick, in
*On the Variation of Reflex Excitability
in the Frog induced by changes of Temperature* (1882).

La grenouille bouillie has been variously applied,
during the Cold War, to relations with the Soviet Union,
by survivalists – at the impending collapse of civilisation –
over inaction to climate change, ribbited
by Al Gore's *An Inconvenient Truth*,
to describe the slow erosion of civil rights,
and even to those who remain
in abusive relationships.
Ad frognitum.

No one ever metaphornicates
about *Rana sylvatica*,
the Alaskan Wood Frog,
able to exist for weeks,
with two-thirds of body water frozen solid,
breath stopped, heart still, waste production halted.
Cryoprotectants help its cells survive.
A frog-shaped block of ice.
Spring-thawed Lazarus.

Whoso Curseth

May your mohel* have a touch of the palsy. (traditional Jewish)

Die, may he: Tiger, catch him; Snake bite him; Steep hill, fall down on him; River, flow over him; Wild boar, bite him. (traditional curse of the Todas of South India)

He should have a large store, and whatever people ask for he shouldn't have, and what he does have shouldn't be requested. (contemporary Jewish)

Cursed be your mother's anus. Cursed be your father's testicles. (traditional Yoruba verbal duelling curse)

May the village matchmaker pair you up with Mel Gibson's distant relative! (contemporary Jewish)

For not letting your parents arrange your marriage, may your babies resemble sloths. (traditional Jewish)

May you grow a long beard and book a vacation in Syria. (traditional Jewish)

May you dig up your father by moonlight and make soup of his bones. (traditional Fiji Islands)

May you wander over the face of the earth forever, never sleep twice in the same bed, never drink water twice from the same well, and never cross the same river twice in a year. (traditional Gypsy)

May your left ear wither and fall into your right pocket. (traditional Arab)

May the worst day of your past be the best day of your future. (traditional Chinese)

Let what I wish on him come true (most, even half, even just 10%). (traditional Jewish)

He should get so sick as to cough up his mother's milk. (traditional Jewish)

His luck should be as bright as a new moon. (traditional Jewish)

He should have Pharaoh's plagues sprinkled with Job's scabies. (traditional Jewish)

---

* A mohel is a Jewish person trained in the practice of *Brit milah* (circumcision).

A Worm's Point of View On Clichés

The early bird catches the worm
is a cliché

but not for the worm.

Bedbug Dreaming

Hundreds of red laser dots
pepper my chest and back
invisible assailants insect ninjas
no whizzing or warning whirrs
bites so unfelt no swat is possible
evolution has taught these
to crawl softly sip shallow
strike and flee
(leaving no trace of pun)

I run my hand over clustered lumps
the child in me connects the dots for a treasure map
the blind Seer senses a lesson in red Braille
the old mystic traces constellations
here Orion there The Dipper
and lower – ah! the Great Jumping Flea.

Birthday

for Lucy Lysenko – June 19

Australopithecus afarensis!
your closest relation
common name: Lucy
age: 3.2 million years old
in Ethiopia called dinknesh the
wondrous one
named by archeologists after
'Lucy in the Sky With Diamonds'
played loudly and repeatedly on the camp tape recorder
…picture yourself in a boat on a river…
her most striking characteristics:
a valgus knee indicating she
normally moved walking upright
a ratio of humerus to femur 84.6%
compared to 71.8% for modern humans
97.8% for common chimpanzees
…with tangerine trees and marmalade skies…
a lumbar curve another indicator of habitual bipedalism
non-pathological flat feet not to be confused with
pes planus (fallen arches)
'Lucy is not the Missing Link' – Dr Richard Leakey
'Lucy in the Sky With Diamonds is not about LSD' – Dr John Lennon
Urban Dictionary: Lucy – a crazy out of this world scheme that usually backfires! Inspired by Lucille Ball's crazy antics on *I Love Lucy*.
…look for the girl with the sun in her eyes and she's gone…
sarcastic malicious dark-haired imp from Peanuts comic strip
who was an absolute bitch to Charlie Brown

…newspaper taxis appear on the shore waiting to take you away…
Gemini exuberant creative
lights up a room when she enters personality
to spare not shy about displaying it
…the girl with kaleidoscope eyes…
others who stole your birthday:
Pascal John Donne
Moe Howard of The Three Stooges
Edward VII's Wallace Simpson
Aung San Suu Kyi
Krishnamurti
Garfield.

Imaginary Gardens Real Toads

No poems can please for long or live that are written by water drinkers. Horace

A poem is never finished, only abandoned. Paul Valery

A poet's autobiography is his poetry. Anything else is just a footnote. Yevtushenko

A poet's work is to name the unnameable, to point at frauds, to take sides, start arguments, shape the world, and stop it going to sleep. Salman Rushdie

All bad poetry springs from genuine feeling. Oscar Wilde

Always be a poet, even in prose. Baudelaire

Children and lunatics cut the Gordian knot which the poet spends his life patiently trying to untie. Cocteau

Each memorable verse of a true poet has two or three times the written content. Alfred de Musset

Even when poetry has a meaning, as it usually has, it may be inadvisable to draw it out. Perfect understanding will sometimes almost extinguish pleasure. A.E. Housman

Genuine poetry can communicate before it is understood. T.S. Eliot

I was reading the dictionary. I thought it was a poem about everything. Steven Wright

If Galileo had said in verse that the world moved the Inquisition might have let him alone. Thomas Hardy

Poetry heals the wounds inflicted by reason. Novalis

Poetry is a deal of joy and pain and wonder, with a dash of the dictionary. Khalil Gibran

Poetry is nearer to vital truth than history. Plato

Poetry is the art of creating imaginary gardens with real toads. Marianne Moore

Poetry is the rhythmical creation of beauty in words. Edgar Allan Poe

Poetry should should strike the reader as a wording of his own highest thoughts, and appear almost a remembrance. John Keats

Poets are soldiers that liberate words from the steadfast possession of definition. Eli Khamarov

The poets have been mysteriously silent on the subject of cheese. Gilbert K. Chesterton

To have great poets there must be great audiences. Walt Whitman

Wanted: a needle swift enough to sew this poem into a blanket. Charles Simic

Poetry is an echo, asking a shadow to dance. Carl Sandburg

Kite

Nothing to write about   not a single idea
Labor's likely rout   or the bluster in Korea
so I simply move pen   a somnambulant stroll
with neither fixed end   nor poetic goal
save to paint ink on page   to exercise the wrist
without beckoning muse mage   or memory's abyss
neither a sonnet's cage   nor a free verse list
just rhyme in the middle   rhyme at the end
merely a fiddle   where the sentence can bend
away from straight prose   or a narrative's spell
it's not one of those   no story to tell
just midnight doggerel   an insomniac's rant
a sleepless inaugural   before I recant
to set aside paper   lay down the pencil
and bid sleep my shaper   with a dream for a stencil
slowing Beta to Alpha   and Alpha to Delta
to slip from the Self   to the place where thoughts melt
dark into light   breaking dawn from the night
a tabula rasa kite   the page again white.

Lost Haiku of Osama Bin Laden

Jihad is merely
dahij with letters backwards
bad Afghani weed

Rude At 4 a.m.

A fully formed poem
woke me up just now.

How rude.

Didn't it see
the do-not-disturb sign
on my writer's block?

The Dr. Seuss That Switched His Voice

'He switched to the Anglicised pronunciation because it "evoked a figure advantageous for an author of children's books".' – Louis Menand

The Dr. Seuss
that switched his voice
did not rejoice

'a flag of truce!
constant misuse
by the obtuse stop
that abuse!

i'm Dr. Seuss!'
His German voice
was much too moist
so Dr. Seuss
made a choice:

'like Mother Goose
now i'm Seuss
as American Seuss
as apple juice!

not Rolls or Royce
not Dr. Soyss

just call me Sewss!
no more excuse

for making noisse
about my voice

so now i choooosh
to introduce
not Bruce or Zeus
but Dr. Seuss!'

The American muuse
found Dr. Seuss
but goosed

the voice
of Doktor Seuss.

A Loon Sang In Walloon

Twice upon a time
when water changed to wine
a loon sang in Walloon
uncertain with her pitch
other loons would twitch
this loon sang out of tune
old loon choirmaster
whose skin was alabaster
and sucked his silver spoon
pucked a sour pooh-pooh
saying this will never do
to have a tin-eared loon
frog said try my ribbit
perhaps you could ad lib it
and croaked a green balloon
the loon soon learned to blend it
its ribbit was quite splendid
there beneath the claret moon
now spiders spread their fingers
fog of sapphire lingers
a loon sang in Walloon.

This Town Ain't Big Enough For Two Giuseppes

Why are professional Italians so bitchy
to other professional Italians in this town?
Who holds the copyright on broken English
and why so twitchy
aren't there enough white fedoras to go around?

Whenever I run into another rooster cacciatore
who earns a crostini peddling Italian *caricatura*
the room seems to shrink
I'm reminded of those lizards who don't blink
with fluttering frill big fan culos spreading the yard
Puffed-Up-R-Us: my card

strutting male chefs really give me the shits
everyone of them hijacking grandma's recipe bits
grandma: who was the consummate amateur
serving up the grandest food *jour après jour*
her whole life she did it for free
for family for love for the art of it for the love of me
she made it herself – every scrap
without all that sous chef crap

Fakirs! Crawl back into your pizza ovens now
come back serving some humility with your ciao

Okay we make a bit of a cartoon of it I admit
but a little kindness from fellow goombas wont kill it

so *pace*
let us break bread and roll bocce
the Mario brothers seem to get along with each other
and Chico Marx had FOUR brothers
(of course that was all really jewish hugs and baci)

and I'm as guilty as the rest of that lot
of this ethno-crime
but take this poem as my mugshot

I'm ready to do my time.

Ulysses For Italians

I guess the man's a genius, but what a dirty mind he has, hasn't he?'
– Nora Joyce (James Joyce's wife, on Molly Bloom's sexy sixty-page monologue at the end of *Ulysses*)

I was a Flower of the mountain no
when I put the rosemary in my hair like
the Calabrian girls used
or shall I wear a red no
and how he kissed me under
the wall and I thought well
as well why him when there's another
and then I asked him with my eyes
to not ask again no
and then he asked me would I no
to say no my garlic blossom
and first I squeezed my hands around
his throat no
and pushed him away from me so
he could feel my breath all onions no
and his heart was going all vafanculo
and no I said no I won't NO!

Lemonscent

The lane neglected in leaf and wrapper
nondescript off the main
save fruit-laden branches peering
over grey board
the old tree stopped me dead
I detoured in pulling the nearest down
snapping the stem others were higher than reach
while looking for something to lift me
I recalled civil law on harvesting fruit
overhanging public lanes: property of owner
still sour sunfaces and green-yellow leers
can't be resisted sliding a wheelie bin balancing shakily
one hand on fence one arm stretching
into thorny light I barely tickled the bottom
rind of a fat one
as the back gate swung open
a lemon-haired woman invited me in
to pick all I wanted
I wouldn't want you to get scratches
helping fill my coat pockets
I like sharing
we touched hands briefly
thanks and goodbye
I left her pleasant lane
returning to a duller street
saturated with scent
of good tidings and lemon.

A Shoe Is a Shoe Is a Shoe

When Prime Minister Julia Gillard
dropped a low-heeled dark blue
Midas Glorify size 36 wedge
at Aboriginal Tent City
it entered Shoe Closet Elysium
with Jesus's thong & Ötzi's frozen-toe binding
every culture slips into shoe fetish
the Egyptian ancient soleless Cleopatra sandal
Masai rawhide & Indian wood
Japanese rice-straw Mexican yucca
Chinese Golden Lily Slippers
today Blahnikt Vuitton Choo
in myth-time Cinderella's Prince
The Old Woman Who Lived in a Shoe
Dorothy's size 6 good-witch ruby slippers
Hans Christian Andersen's whirling reds
brought madness to dancers
Gods and Heroes wore none
Alexander the Great had barefoot armies
a person of great wealth was well-heeled
16th century royalty introducing the high heel
court ladies appearing larger-than-life
while Persian horsemen claimed high heels helped hold
riders' feet in stirrups
cones kittens puppies spools stilettos
Evdokia Petrova's lost grey clog on the Mascot tarmac
newspapered incorrectly as a Commie Red
suggested instead emerging Australian womenpower
air hostess Joyce Bull lending Petrova her own

Khrushchev banged a good low one in protest
forcing UN officials to turn off his microphone
but granddaughter Nina said he only removed them
because they were too tight Nikita's son Sergie
denied it happened at all claiming no photo proof
anyway papa was too big and couldn't reach his feet.

Last-minute Gift Ideas For the Cheating Ex-

a bullet with her/his name on it
a bullet with the other bastard/bitch's name on it
a bullet with your name on it

(who said jealousy can't be funny?)

or

if you're feeling clever and sobriquet
you could give the collected set.

In the Manner of Cavafy

Certainly Petrius   achieves a somewhat similar
tone of voice   the historical perspective
his unexpected   humour often dividing lines
for emphasis   in the manner of the master
(as this poem   demonstrates by illustration
the beguilement   of the technique)
but Petrius   is not a master
too timid to   step out onto the parapet
into the brightness   of his true self
he remains content   to huddle there in shadow
donning the discarded personae   of the teacher
like a child   in a party costume

do not be deceived Yorgos   by his standing
in academia   his reputation
amongst men of letters   the accolades accumulated
the fine journal   he edits
these are illusions   his poems are forgotten
almost as soon   as they are written

Petrius is a pretender   content to remain
in the shade   of a great writer
too timid to venture out   onto the terrifying parapet.

Jolokia

The ghost
Indian's cruellest chili pepper
four hundred times the punch of Tabasco
Guinness Record's hottest until
superseded in 2012 by Trinidad Scorpion
nicknamed Noga after ferocious Naga warriors
Bih Jolokia the poison Jolokia
the mighty chili the rough chili
ripe peppers coloured red
orange yellow chocolate
a food a spice a relief from sunheat
weaponised by the Indian Army
a tear gas grenade for mob control rioters and terrorists
imparting distinctive flavour to curries chutneys
smeared on fences in Northern India
will repel wild elephants.

Masturbari

Egyptian God Atun created the universe by masturbating to
 ejaculation
the ebb and flow of the Nile attributed to the frequency of his
 orgasms
Pharaohs henceforth paid tribute ceremoniously spilling seed
 into the river water
ancient Greeks called female self-touching anaphlam up-fire
Sixteenth century onanism was commonly practised
by nannies to put young male wards to sleep
Tissot in the Eighteenth argued semen an essential oil
when lost from the body reduced memory blurred vision
 caused gout
disturbance of appetite and weak-mindedness his theories
 adopted by Voltaire
and Kant – who considered masturbari a violation of moral
 law contributed
to its consideration over the next two centuries
as mental illness by medicine self-pollution sin and vice by
 religion
resulting in chastity belts straight jackets cauterisation often
 surgical excision of genitals
Victorian schoolboys were advised to have pants
constructed so private parts could not be touched through
 pockets
schoolgirls arranged at special desks to discourage crossing legs
forbidden the riding of horses or bicycles to prevent sensations
physicians supplied Strengthening Tinctures and Prolific
 Powders
bland meatless diets were promoted by Dr John Kellogg
inventor of cornflakes

the Reverend Sylvester Graham inventor of the Cracker
turn-of-the-century seamstresses discovered
sitting near the edge of the treadle seat delivered rewards
the Scout Association who in 1914 advised boys to run away
 from temptations
recanted in 1930 considering it a natural act and abstinence an
 error
in recent times the UK National Health Service slogan:
An Orgasm a Day Keeps the Doctor Away encouraged teens to
 practise once daily
to stem youth pregnancy the Spanish region of Extremadura
distributed leaflets: Pleasure is in Your Hands
current theory shows regular activity lowers probability of
 prostate cancer
reduces coronary heart disease in males over fifty improves
 sperm motility and health
if practised by women before coitus increases fertility relieves
 depression
leads to higher self-esteem increased relaxation and better sleep
sperm banks in the US are known as masturbatoriums.

Distant Relations

The box spring squeals,
through the plasterboard,
a rusty iron heartbeat.
In the children's dark bedroom,
during pause in the 3 a.m. concert,
alert unshuttered eyes
stare at imagined shapes.

My father's voice: *are you ready?*
My mother's: *I'm rarin' to go.*
The love engine begins rolling.
Suddenly, from the bed next to mine,
my little brother scalds
our scared silence.
Mommy, what are you DOING?
I hold my breath,
fearful of beatings.
It's all right, honey, go back to sleep.
I choke a nervous giggle.

In the morning, after dad goes off, nosing
through bathroom wastebasket,
I find a crumpled ball of toilet tissue –
inside, the tied-off French letter,
full of mercury.
A jewel in a baby's sock.
It jiggles in my small hand.
I feel akin.

Music 101

I attribute my unerring sense of rhythm,
the accuracy at which I am able to play,
dead on beat, to my mother's skill,
with the pasta spoon.

Bent over her aproned lap,
for one digression or another,
she brought the heavy wooden baton
down onto my backside,
like a skilled German conductor.

I – told – you – not – to – do – that

One word per strike, metrical,
marrying forever, pain, and precision,
word and rhythm.

Don't – ev – er – let – me – catch – you – do – ing – that – a – gain

Short, sharp, per – cuss – ive, Protestant words.

I was blessed she never knew the value
of a thesaurus.

Robin Hood Roulette

'I shot an arrow into the air.' – Longfellow

When I was thirteen,
my brother, eleven,
and I would take my bow,
and metal-tipped arrows,
to the local track oval,
to play one of our secret
dangerous games.

Launching a shaft
straight up, until
we lost sight of it,
having no idea where
it would land,
no place to shelter,
blessedly free,
we zigzagged and screamed,
ecstatically terrified, surrendering
to our hurtling feathered fate.

Shuffleboard

Sawdust-sprinkled floors smelling of spilt lager
grown-ups sitting on swivel stools
the bar lit fairground-bright
spirit bottles toy umbrellas in triangle glasses
red Maraschino cherry green toothpicked olive
an uncle owned the beer joint near the negro
railroad tracks my mother and father
brought us kids for Friday night perch dinner
while waiting for meals my favourite time
was playing the room length 22-foot shuffleboard
a smooth slick narrow table top shooting polished
steel hockey puck discs down a waxed surface
unknowingly sliding time

in 15th century England it was groat
large silver pennies were pushed
during the American Revolution
English soldiers and Colonialists played variations
Knock Off, Horse Collar and Crazy Eight
throws included Hangers and Corners
not scoring constituted a Hickey
bets were placed in the Hickey Jar
played in back rooms during the Depression and Prohibition
it left and returned with GIs during World War II
Hollywood embraced it in the fifties
Betty Grable and Harry James had custom-built inlaid tables
hitting or shaking the board was not allowed
shooters kept one foot behind playing surface when sliding
rules required players to shake hands before and after a match
no drinks or cigarettes allowed in hands or mouth while playing

a serious gamer brought his own personalised set of steel pucks
sand once used to speed the board evolved
into fine corn and silicone wax
shuffling became almost extinct during the electronic game age
but is making a slow and steady climb back

Pee Wee Ramos is one of twelve members
inducted into the National Shuffleboard Hall of Fame
some years ago before my father died
he took me back to the old beer joint by the negro tracks
Friday night was still perch night
the local-caught fish was as good as I remembered
the shuffleboard was gone.

Thirty-three Years of Bliss

an anniversary meditation

33 is the largest positive integer that cannot be expressed as a sum of different triangular numbers

a normal human spine has 33 vertebrae

the divine name Elohim appears 33 times in the story of creation

Jesus's age when he was crucified in 33 A.D.

a religious image of the Virgin Mary from the 18th century is known in Uruguay as *Virgen de los Treinta y Tres* (Virgin of the Thirty-Three)

according to Al-Ghazali, the dwellers of Heaven will exist eternally in a state of being age 33

Islamic prayer beads are generally arranged in sets of 33

33s are long-playing records or LPs

in French Italian Romanian Spanish and Portuguese the word a patient is usually asked to say when a doctor is listening to his or her lungs with a stethoscope – *Trente-trois*, *Trentatrè*, *Treizeci și trei*, *Treinta y tres* and *Trinta e três*

the number of workers trapped and also the number of survivors of the 2010 Copiapó mining accident

Alexander the Great died at the age of 33

the atomic number of arsenic

33 is – according to the Newton scale – the temperature at which water boils.

Apparition

Something not right woke me from my dreaming.
The cold air, perhaps a premonition?
In the dark, I listened for your breathing.

Tonight in your own bed, you were sleeping,
Beyond my care, my touch, my cognition.
Something not right woke me from my dreaming.

I tiptoed stairs, in the doorway leaning,
(you went to bed in such sad condition).
In the dark, I listened for your breathing.

Windblown curtain. Things not what they're seeming,
Life-without-you awful apparition,
Something not right woke me from my dreaming.

The rise and fall of your breast, so pleasing,
Call it just some midnight superstition,
Something not right woke me from my dreaming,
In the dark, I listened for your breathing.

Short Wave

The voices of our three granddaughters
far off down the creek blurred and jumbled
laughter swallowed by wind
fragments squawking a short wave radio
now in tune now out
I can almost make out words in static
then the dial moves and crow song and bird whistle
retune frequencies to the breeze.

The Daughter That Still Loves Me

One out of two isn't bad.
I haven't spoken to her brother for thirty years.
She and I don't see each other that often – on all
the major family-love days: birthdays, Christmas,
Father's Day. (Sometimes
she forgets, but,
under the circumstances, that's ok – the split
with her mother was ugly.)

But I think she has forgiven me
for abandoning her, or however kids
view separation, when one parent has to go.

My daughter loves me and I love her.
We never got divorced.

Arl

The first memorable thing
about my accountant Arl
he precisely tapped the large calculator keys
with his right hand without looking once
eyes fixed to the left on my pencil-scribbled figures
his error-free tally finished
he pulled a Zippo out
give me all the cash in your wallet he said
why? I asked
It is completely unnecessary to pay all this tax
so you might as well burn the money now
later I discovered he was a practising Catholic
a volume of Martin Luther King's
Strength to Love pride-of-place
amongst tax and law tomes
Arl invited me to his Malvern home
for early Monday morning training sessions
escorted quickly through a hardly lived in mansion
in the rear garden was a fully functioning boxing ring
Arl taught me a martial arts kata he invented
based on the Sign of the Cross
one step forward edge of right hand out and straight up

in the name of the Father

one step backward edge of hand down to waist

and of the Son

(he was an elegant mantis)
small step forward hand passing to the left

and of the Holy…

step backwards hand passing to the right

...Ghost...

both hands together head bowed

Amen

warmed up he suddenly tossed me
a pair of red boxing gloves
put these on and get in the ring
ok now hit me as hard as you can
I don't feel like hitting you
no its ok hit me he insisted
lightly punching me in the shoulder
so I poked him a couple of times
sort of sparring but make-believe
not like fighting off
my father as a child which was for real
some months later Arl told me he was retiring
sold his house and vanished
I never saw him again
a mutual friend confided that Arl had given
up one of his wealthier Sydney clients
to the Tax Department in exchange for immunity
the businessman had a contract out on him
a Maori heavy once told me
there is only one way to deal with conmen: physical violence
I don't know if there's any truth to the story
I don't know if Arl was a genius or a crook
but I miss him and his strange mind
I have a more conservative accountant now
I sleep better
he hasn't encouraged me to punch him yet.

Ode Al Dente

'The gods send nuts to those who have no teeth.' – proverb

My jaw aches and a drowsy numbness pains,
safe in my bed, far from the dentist's chair,
as nerves shake off the spell of Novocain,
I gaze upon this wrenched tooth resting there,

upon my palm, like Hamlet might have stared,
its crack, exiting from the cementum,
still echoing like gunshot in my ears.

The tooth, now separated from my care,
yanked from a bloody gum,
I would reflect awhile upon its cheer.

It's said George Washington had wooden teeth,
but now they claim history was misled –
a frightening set of dentures served his needs,
of metal, gold, animal fangs and lead.

From Medicine, Dentistry was distinct,
once practised by the barbers and blacksmiths.
The first toothbrushes were cinnamon sticks.

Now, 3-D stamps out new fake teeth, by links –
aesthetic ceramics –
from online templates, broken teeth are fixed.

The hardest substance in our human home.
The longest lasting fossil in the frame.
Multiple layers of tissue – not bone –
fingerprint-unique, no two are the same.

Asleep, beneath milk tooth diphyodont,
the rise to permanence, in jaw, with me,
for longer years, than any wife or friend,

it could outlast this poem, to be quite blunt,
in Archaeology,
this molar might define me, in the end.

If Hitler Also Spelled Hiedler

Hüttler or Huettler
at seventeen had remained
in watercolour been accepted
at the Academy of Fine Arts Vienna
even become a priest as once intended
the swastika would still signify
auspiciousness in Sanskrit
Israel wouldn't exist
no Berlin or West Bank walls
holocaust would refer to
a burnt offering of Moses
World War I would still be the Great War
I would have had one more uncle.

Blondi

Eva Braun preferred her Scottish terriers,
Negus and Stasi, and hated Blondi,
whom she secretly kicked under tables,
getting satisfaction when Hitler became perplexed
at the shepherd's strange behaviour.

Goebbels said the Führer enjoyed walking Blondi,
certain of no conversation on war or politics.

Blondi had five whelps,
one named Wulf,
after the Latin meaning of Adolph –
adalwolf: noble wolf.

Blondi, propaganda star,
portrayed the Führer as animal lover,

but doubting potency,
of the final cyanide capsules,
Hitler ordered one
tested on Blondi,

who died instantly.

Can You Write Left-Handed Poetry?

The clerk at the Schreibstube produced
samples on a paper pad:
gutter rhymes, obscenities, filthy limericks.
Eighteen-year-old Abraham Cykiert
had written verse since fourteen,
but, in Auschwitz, a good poem earned
extra soup, bread. Even shoes.

Cykiert wrote the doggerel well,
becoming a member of a group,
that amused capos and SS at camp functions.
The Nazis loved his filth, and laughed.
At the end of the night, the entertainers
were rewarded with party leftovers,

but after the war, Abraham Cykiert
was so ashamed of the left-handed poetry
he had written to survive,
it took him twenty years
before he could write
anything
else.

Kilroy

was here.

The world's most well-known
graffito. Bald-headed geezer
with banana-nose peeping over walls,
fingers clutching sides to steady a pea-eyed gaze.

In World War II, the average Joe's
default method of planting the flag,
on every available wall, barn, railway carriage.
Discovered on so much captured US weaponry,
Hitler thought it a code name.
Even Stalin found Kilroy
perving in his bathroom.

Known as Mr Chad in the UK,
Private Snoops, The Goon and Watcher.
A variety of accompanying slogans included:
Wot, no sugar?
Wot, no Führer?
In World War I Australia, Foo Was Here.
In Africa, Smoe & Clem.
In Russia, Vasya.
Other nicknames: Flywheel, The Jeep,
Luke the Spook and Stinkie.

Contests held to discover origins
How Kilroy Got There
to no avail.
One theory suggested a derivation
of Greek Omega Ω
the symbol for electrical resistance.

In 1997, the little witness was
last officially spotted
peeking over the edge
of New Zealand stamp # 1422.

The earliest documented version, 1937,
chalk-scratched inside
Fort Knox.

War and Peace Senryu

for Myron Lysenko

That bastard Pierre.
Pierre marries Natasha.
(Tolstoy drinks vodka.)

The Jimmy Leg

The torso arm the phantom limb
the itch that just won't segue
the ticklings that refuse to stop
you got the Jimmy Leg

the urge to move the antsy
the pin and needle flag
the fall asleep sciatica
you got the Jimmy Leg

the restless and abrupt totter
a circadian rhythm lag
the Parkinson nod and wag
you got the Jimmy Leg

the leaping and contractions
the daytime sleepy nag
a crawling feeling in the skin
you got the Jimmy Leg

the sudden jolt wide awake
the sleep depriving dreg
the narcolepsy powder keg
you got the Jimmy Leg

the hypnic twist around and jerk
the sleep-loss twitching rag
the fall into oblivion
you got the Jimmy Leg.

Reconciliation Haiku

Ugly words were said.
Words that had no business in
the mouths of lovers.

Of course I was right,
but the smug way I was right
was completely wrong.

I'm sorry I said
words of any weight or length.
Silence was required.

Petrolhead Zen

after Gary Snyder

Drinking the neck and shoulders
off a bottle of Johnny Walker Red

cleaning and sharpening the chainsaw

there is no other life.

Lorca Said I Can Conceive

Lorca said *I can conceive
of no poetry other than the lyric*
the rhythm the rhyme the weave
of song so why then do we fear it
jump-rope tunes lullabies
refrains of childhood games
the fee fo the fum and fi
a sing-a-long with Dick and Jane
Spot and Cousin George
Dr. Seuss Mother Goose
the Three Bears steaming porridge
Bullwinkle the Moose
cartoons nonsense doggerel
have informed who we are
bless Ogden Nash and Lewis Carroll
When You Wish Upon a Star
Picasso said it took him five
years to paint like Raphael
but a whole life he had to strive
to tell the stories a child can tell
so sing up the country lullaby
and remember ourselves to sleep
forget about Almighty Why:
in the simple lay the deep.

Letter From the King

If I blow a hundred,
And Charles wears the Ring,
Will I be receiving
A Letter from the King?

A Special Court telegram,
With Royal cheer and laughter
On my 100th, 105th,
And every birthday after,

And if I drew a lucky gene,
And call in all my bets,
I'll get a swag of Kingly letters,
I could collect the set.

But just the sound of it is awful,
It somehow feels all wrong,
Like Lord Godiva side-saddle,
Or Fay Wray and Queen Kong.

A postcard from HER Majesty.
Now that's the proper gift,
(Although the custom started
Way back with George V.)

No, not much to look forward to,
A Letter from the King.

No matter how you say it,
It doesn't have the ring.

If Good News Sold Newspapers

If good news sold newspapers
murder would make page 3
as headlines shouted VLAD PUTIN
HAD TWO BLINTZS TODAY WITH TEA
Bulletin Just In: THE SUN
IS PERFECTLY ROUND AGAIN
paparazzi would photograph lovers
holding hands along the Seine
Politics compressed as an insert
in the middle and never repeated
or recycled as wrapping for fish & chips
for any who much cared to read it
the serial killers and rapists
expensive bottles of Grange
would never even rate a banner
just a box on the crosswords page
pasty-faced brokers and businessmen
with ponzi schemes and lies
would go after the cartoon strips
or be buried in Classifieds

now imagine poetry as Breaking News!
on Page One: Chagall and Boyd
if good news sold newspapers
we'd all be less paranoid.

I Set a Mousetrap Late Last Night

I set a mousetrap late last night
with a cube of wholemeal bread
by morning light I soon discovered
I'd caught a broom instead

my wife must have leaned it there
in that corner unaware
yet and still the bread was gone
I had no notion where

about an hour or so ago
after a bottle of wine
silent-gazing at the fire
with nothing on my mind

I saw a mouse head poking
out of the firewood sticks
our beady eyes quickly met
I almost read his lips

he seemed to be enquiring
if tonight I would be serving
the bread and broom combo again
his boldness was unnerving

I recognised immediately
a fellow philosopher
and agreed to break bread cordially
again with him (or her)

the same table as before I asked
the corner of the room
he'd find his bread cube on the tray
this time without the broom.

The Rime of the Ancient Gooney Bird

The land of water, and of fearful hunger, where no swimming creature was to be hooked or crooked.	The fish were here, the fish were there, The fish were all about: Our hunger growled, and churned and howled, But fish we had caught nought!
A great sea-fowl, called the Gooney Bird, comes through the fog, lured by the sailors.	At length I saw a Gooney Bird, 5 Fly o'er the foggy rip, As though it were a Columbidae, We lured it with a chip.
The Gooney Bird returneth regularly for a daily snack.	A good South Wind rung up like rhyme; 9 The Gooney Bird did dance, And every day, for potato cakes, Came down as in a trance!
The Gooney Bird chokes on a cast-off rollie, mistaken for a morsel.	One day it swallowed a fag-butt whole, 13 Lodged sideways in its throat, The bird spun round delirious And fell dead on the boat.
The hungry crew endeavour to prepare the stubborn fowl for tea.	We plucked all day and boiled all night, 17 Tight-lipped without a word. 'God save my Auntie's marinade!' The fowl was tough as curd.
The sailors reluctantly, eat the foul fowl, using available shipboard condiments, and thus, are saved.	Its thigh was stubborn as a boot, 21 The flavour quite absurd, But with a side of chips and sauce, We ate that GOONEY BIRD.

Chicago Typewriter

Great-granddaddy of the
AK-47 aka Chicago Piano
Organ Grinder Trench Broom
Chopper Tommy
the Anti-Bandit Gun
favoured for its ergonomics
wooden furniture parts
.45-calibre type C drum magazine
designed by General John T. Thompson
for World War I (which ended
before production began)
early models offered to the public
suffered poor sales priced at 200 dollars
compared to 400 for a Model-T
first serious customers US Postal Service
Mafia Irish Republic Greek Gendarmerie
infamous during Prohibition (yes the ones in violin cases)
mass-produced for World War II
saw action in Tobruk the Greek Civil War
in the 1948 Arab–Israeli Conflict
the Chicago Typewriter was carried by both sides
one sold at auction in 2012 for 130,000 dollars
previous owners Bonnie & Clyde.

Chess Player

'Pawns are the soul of chess.' – Philidor, World Chess Champion, Paris, 1773

I visited Estonia just
after the Soviets left
liberation tactile.
300,000 voices strong,
a Singing Revolution,
brought a quarter of all Estonians
into Talinn Arena for strictly
forbidden national songs and hymns.

On the street schnitzels &
boiled potatoes cost a dollar,
the depleted local grocery
had two cabbages & a few beetroots.

I found a rare and magnificent old
Russian chess set in a second-hand shop.
After paying $100 cash to a red-bearded
Goliath reclining in half-shadow
behind the counter I heard
him sneer in broken
English

> *I don't need little pieces.*
> *I play you in head.*

You could have heard a pawn
drop.

I suspect he was loath to sell
the precious old set.

Skeptic's Friday

A black ladder crossed my path,
I walked under a cat.
Broken luck, seven-year mirror,
when in church, leave on your hat.
Knock off wood. Finger Crosses.
The thirteenth elevator cuts your losses.
Shoe a horse, pointing up,
spill the salt, in someone's lap.
Put a table on your shoes.
Closed umbrellas, outdoors, can't lose.

Spock

Original Dutch family name Spaak,
fur traders, settled the 17th century American colony
of New Netherlands.

Second wife, Mary, forty years younger,
introduced Spock to macrobiotic living –
he continued racing sailboats until
the age of eighty-four.

Norman Vincent Peale claimed
Dr Spock's child-rearing books
led to the anti-Vietnam War movement.
Permissiveness in youth.

Son, Michael, directed
the Boston Children's Museum.
Grandson, Peter, 22, committed suicide,
jumping off the museum roof.

A mother once wrote him,
Thank God, I've never used your horrible book.
That's why my children take baths,
wear clean clothes,
and get good grades in school.

Leechcraft

Egyptians used leeches
3,500 years ago, painting
them into hieroglyphics
(at first, mistakenly, thought to be cobras).
The Roman physician Galen
popularised leeching, announcing
major arteries filled with blood, not
air, as previously believed.
Leeches are hermaphroditic segmented worms,
with six to eight pairs of legs,
and thirty-two brains, one per segment.
A staple in Middle Age home medicine cabinets,
if a leech refused to drink,
it could be encouraged with ale.
A family doctor was commonly referred to,
both professionally, and respectfully, as
the Leech.

Tick

Itchy little skin flap.
On closer look,
a tick, pincered in tight.
In the microscope's stare,
a Haller's organ, sensored
tarus, twitching
for breath, body odour, vibration.
Haematophagic nano-Nosferatu,
with nothing eternal to swap,
offering Lyme's and Haemorrhagic.
Cousin of mite,
great-grandbug of Cretaceous,
incapable of jump or glide,
eight-legged aerial artist of leaf & stem,
questing for the blood animal of me.
Low temperatures kill them.
Guinea fowls munch them –
two birds can clear two acres in a year.

Agony Aunts

A custom begun as eighteenth century
question-answer column for men,
until a gentlewoman, asking if ladies
could also submit inquires, was assured
her questions would be taken seriously.

UKs best known, Dear Marge,
was Rebecca Marjorie Proops OBE.
Almost as popular, mid-wife Claire Rayner,
referred to as the opposite of a shrinking violet –
a swollen rhododendron,
even described herself as a stubborn old bag,
offering her signature empathy:
done it myself, lovey.

For anonymity, readers often
adjective-signed letters –
Sincerely, Confused.

Fictional Mrs Mills, of the *Sunday Times*,
gave humorous bad advice: get a new best friend –
she is obviously sleeping with your husband.

In the US, Ask Ann Landers (aka Ruth Crowley),
lived on, after her death, in
Esther 'Eppie' Pauline Friedman Lederer,
who won the column, in a contest.

Eppie's twin sister, Pauline Esther 'Popo' Phillips,
(who said marriage must be permanent,
even when disturbed by masculine lunacy),
started Dear Abby,
permanently estranging the twins.

Obviously, they never wrote each other for advice.

Nachtmahr

Not horse, but demon,
goblin-like hobbling, of dreaming,
bat-leathery sarcoma,
exploding the sleep-cave.
I snap awake, as from a coma,
crawling out of fear-grave,
staggering, blind,
zombie shuffling, anywhere,
wanting to hurt someone, in kind,
narrowed in nightmare,
grabbing a phantom shirt, ready to punch
can't stop, retreat,
standing still, hunched,
untwisting my twisted sheet.
This house is queer, the bedroom scares,
I don't want to go back in there.
I calm myself, straddle a chair,
I write something down, writing deep,
writing myself steeply back to sleep.

Noh Means Noh

Coffee is a girl who never tells a boy Noh.
Never take Noh for an answer.
Sometimes Noh is the kindest word.
There's Noh place like home.
Noh pain, Noh gain.
Noh harm, Noh foul.
Noh way, José.
Where there is Noh vision, the people perish.
See Noh evil, hear Noh evil, speak Noh evil.
Noh Vacancy.
Noh Standing.
Noh child left behind.
Noh worries.
Noh man's land.
Noh annual fee.
The Pub With Noh Beer.
Initially… Noh.
Noh BS.
Long time Noh see.
Noh is a complete sentence.

Noh.

(What part of Noh don't you understand?)

Breakaleg

The New Statesman, in 1921, declared theatre
the second most superstitious institution
in England, after horse racing.
To wish luck was unlucky.
Theories of origin abound.
Old slang for a bow, or curtsy, at curtain call.
Elizabethan audiences banged chairs
for approval, often until a leg broke.
Ancient Greeks didn't applaud, they stomped,
and if one stomped hard enough…
German World War I pilots wished each other
hals und beinbruch – neck and leg fractures.
Lincoln Theory holds assassin
John Wilkes Booth broke his
leaping from the balcony.
French *acteurs* declare *Merde!*
'The Divine Sarah' Bernhardt only had one leg,
so good luck, to be like her.
The Italian *attore* encourages
in *bocca a lupo* –
into the mouth of the wolf –
with a reply essential,
before placing a foot on the stage,
crepi il lupo –
may the wolf die.

A Charming Bath

after Elizabeth Smither

After work has grown sour,
and sun's a drooping flower,
      with mauve clouds in its path,
don't look up at that shower –
      just run a charming bath.

Now, showers get you started,
when sleep leaves you fainthearted,
      to face a workday's wrath,
but mystic calm uncharted,
      flows from a charming bath.

As end of day befuddles,
and mind gets wired and muddled,
      the soul is stuffed with math,
climb in the steaming puddle
      of a charming salted bath.

Spellbound, immersed in water,
receive the imprimatur
      of that holiest of paths,
just make it slightly hotter,
      sink in a charming bath.

When family seems so dour,
stay in an extra hour,
      read poems by Sylvia Plath.
Your thoughts will be empowered,
      within a charming bath.

Don't buy Latin prescriptions,
throw wobblies or conniptions,
        pay psychics, telepaths.
Repose, like some Egyptian,
        in a claw-foot charming bath.

Ice Ann

Let me tell you   all   about Ice Ann.
She had one ice eye,   and one ice hand,
Her teeth were cold,   her lips were nice,
But everything she bit   turned into ice.

I met Ice Ann   on an ice blind date,
We fell in love,   but it turned to hate,
I loved her body,   I learned too late,
She was way below zero,   in her mental state.

I married Ice Ann   in a tall ice church,
Exchanged ice rings,   but it could have been worse,
Ice Ann's mother   made a big ice cake,
I ate so much   that I started to shake.

Our wedding night   was snowy treat,
We slept beneath   her fine ice sheet.
She gave me a kiss   and an ice back rub.
We made love twice   in an old ice tub.

Well, I fell into   a deep ice sleep,
And dropped down a hole,   six feet deep,
The slides were slippery,   I couldn't climb out,
My throat was frozen,   and I couldn't shout.

I dreamt we had   two little ice twins.
One looked like me,   I looked like him.
The other grabbed my ear,   with a frosty claw,
She was the spitting image   of her old ice ma.

I woke up suddenly,   in an ice-cold sweat,
Ice Ann was standing there,   soaking wet.
Her nightie was ripped,   she looked a wreck,
She was holding an ice pick   over my neck.

I called 99,   they sent the ice man,
He drove her away,   in his big ice van.
But the fuel line froze,   the steering jammed,
He hit a gumtree,   and killed Ice Ann.

So we laid her out,   in her favourite freezer,
Called on the Reverend   Ebenezer,
For the Final Rites,   he raised the Host,
To the Hailstone Mary,   and the Frozen Ghost.

We stacked Ann's body,   on a funeral pyre,
She was so damned cold,   she froze the fire.
We poured on petrol,   but she wouldn't burn,
So an ice cube tray,   was her makeshift urn.

Instead of ashes,   we shaved Ice Ann,
And crammed her flakes   in an old tin can,
I hired a plane,   and flew it myself,
And scattered her over   the Larsen Shelf.

They say the ocean   rose that day,
A piece of glacier   just broke away,
Polar bears jumped   right off and swam,
To get away   from cold Ice Ann.

An eskimo paddling   a red kayak,
Pulled alongside   the floating pack.
He took his axe,   gave it a whack,
And stuck Ice Ann,   in his sealskin sack.

He traded Ice Ann,   at the Trading Post,
For a pack of tobacco,   and a Walrus roast.
The trading fellas   packed Ice Ann,
In a tuna crate,   bound for Japan.

Now, Hari Sakamoto was eating sashimi,
When he suddenly got the heebie-jeebies.
He started coughing, and couldn't chew,
He choked and spit, and turned bright blue.

They wheeled him down to the Emergency Ward,
He was cold as hell, stiff as a board.
They switched the defibrillator up flat chat,
Ice Ann jumped out, mad as a cat!

They say when a butterfly flaps its wings,
A tsunami blows, in East Peking.
When Ice Ann bit down with her teeth,
It whitened a section of the Barrier Reef.

She bit the nurse, she bit the doctor,
She bit the defibrillator, that really shocked her,
She bit her way, through the hospital wall,
And left an ice tunnel, three feet tall.

Now, I know this tale sounds convoluted,
But Ice Ann got reconstituted.
She hired a limo, and a Swiss chauffeur,
And was looking for me, the last I heard.

So, let me tell you all about Ice Ann,
She had one ice eye, and one ice hand,
Her teeth were cold, her lips were nice,
But everything she bit turned into ice.

Bonyi

Bidwilli.
Jurassic cousin of the Monkey Puzzle.
They live five hundred years.
Watermelon-sized 10 kilograms spiked
green cones, four to a tree.

Known, unaffectionately,
as conck-ya-pines,
a couple was hospitalised by a cone
in Nelson Queen's Gardens.
Another killed a cockatoo in Parramatta.
A big one, nicknamed Titanic,
fell sixty feet and flattened a horse.
Windscreens, roofs and bonnets
are regularly entertained.

Maton has been carving guitar headboards
from Bunya pine for twenty years.

Aboriginals eat the shoots,
peel the bark for kindling.
Nuts are consumed raw,
boiled, barbecued or roasted,
(in the latter, a drilled hole avoids explosions),
flavour of starchy potato and chestnut,
gluten-free, makes a red tea.

Ideal for bonsai.

Sandmen

The quartet of saffron-robed
monks huddle the ring
like back alley dice-players,
throwing for reincarnation stakes.
Tiny tin funnels siphon coloured grains
along pre-chalked template of mandala.
With painstaking patience, over days,
the dazzling pattern emerges until
it is finally complete.

                Without hesitation,
a firm broom sweep disperses it back
to formlessness, symbolising
the fragility and impermanence of matter,
(or transitory nature of the works of man,
                for that matter),
but not before dozens of tourists' cameras
take a stab at digital immortality.

Ceremony over, the Tibetan men retire
to cigarettes, while novices shovel
discarded blue, rose, green, white and black
still-quite-permanent sand
into tin buckets, and toss
it into bins, where it settles down
amongst organic scraps and coffee grounds.

Meanwhile, on the Nile,
under unforgiving heat,
the Great Sphinx of Giza,
The Terrifying One,
also sifted into shape,
from similar mettle,
by equally focused sand-blown men,
(poor Buddhists, no doubt, but perhaps
better craftsmen),
growls its low five-thousand-year Om.

Pokie Poem

Four in the morning,   liver hour break,
the gallstones feel radioactive,   ache,
not enough for   a complete meltdown,
but sore enough,   to push me around
some bad news   dream –
I jolt awake,   mid-scene.

Probing dark,   for the kitchen light,
I sit idly on toilet,   sleep-sight
thumbing food magazines,   Vogue,
then stand there,   transfixed by the stove,
contemplating a snack,   or forgotten name,
saucepan of water   on the flame,
the cracked cup,   the teaspoon tool,
the sugar, milk,   tea-bag ritual.

Still too nightmare-wired   to sleep,
so over to the bookcase,   a blank stare sweep,
scanning titles,   shelf after shelf,
praying for a volume,   to announce itself,
like playing pokies,   some Three-Cherry read.
Soon, out of coin,   back in bed, with my tea,
sitting before this blank paper,   I bow,
with pencil in hand, well…   not blank now.

Evil Eye

'For a man to fear the gay male gaze,
is to fear the Evil Eye or, rather, the Evil Not-I,
the dissolution of self in narcissistic looking.' – Ellis Hanson

Great-great-great grandmother of Lacan's Anxious Gaze,
Mulvey's Male Gaze and the Nosferatu Predatory Gaze,
known in every culture – the Curse
cast by a malevolent stare.
Referred to in Plato, Plutarch and Pliny.
Traditional tribal wariness of those with green, or blue, eyes.
In Italy, *Jettatore*, high arching brows, a fixed look
that leaps from black sockets.
(Pius IV was known for his.)
Mak Pilau, in Hawaiian, rotten eyes, a ghost.
In Brazil, *Olho Gordo*, fat eye.
In Somali, *Qumayo*, envy eye.
Mal de Ojo, in Spain – the traditional cure:
a raw chicken egg, broken into a glass of water,
placed under the bed, if the yolk appears
cooked, the patient recovers.
Nazar, in Islam. Reading the last three chapters
of the Koran will ward it off, or a small black cloth, hung
from the bumper of your truck.
Often mistaken for the thousand-yard stare of battle-weary soldiers.
Also known as Stink Eye, Skunk Eye,
the Hairy Eyeball.

Natte Yallock Jump Rope

Milkbar's gone, pub is shut,
older kids now catch the bus,
half an hour away they go,
the bigger school in Marysborough.

> Ring-a-round the rosie,
> the local school is closing,
> Natte Yallock, what a shame –
> Big Water Little Plain.

Sing a song in gibberish rhyme,
turn the rope in perfect time,
one each end, one jumps between,
children growing in their green.

Budget cut, teachers go,
three small children in a row,
the last ones in the dying town,
no new families coming now.

School, school, Golden Rule,
spell your name and go to school,
mister minister, please tell me,
what our future's going to be?

> Ring-a-round the rosie,
> the local school is closing,
> Natte Yallock, what a shame –
> Big Water Little Plain.

Where Is the Poetry In Pain?

Where is the poetry in pain,
when one has to suffer so much?
How can mere words keep you sane,
when a touch is needed to touch

those places where language can't go?
Someone to protect you from harm
or bandage the bruise that won't show.
Someone to embrace in your arms

and lay for awhile with you there,
listening as you breathe, or cry,
reminding you someone still cares
whether you live or you die.

But, if no kind one is near,
a poem, that is honest, just might
supply a map for the fear,
to steady you down from the height,

loosen the wire where you're caught,
give latitude lines for bearing,
a moment to focus your thought
or a sympathy card of caring.

There is no poetry in pain.
Someone who's lost – or who's missed –
poetry can never regain.
Poems keep you company, at best.

Voltaire Left

I may not agree with what you say,
but I will attack, to your death,
for my Right not to hear it.

The Days of Real Door-to-door Are Done

The days of real door-to-door are done.
Once knocks brought encyclopedias,
sidings, thick wall carpets heralding
wise men with camels, proud stags.
Strangers, in white shirts and ties,
speaking rapidly through screen doors,
of libraries and vacuums.
They squeezed inside for demonstrations.
NO! meant keep talking.

At ten, I was consigned to accordion,
a black-buttoned rental for rehearsal.
I poked 'Three Blind Mice'
for three blind months, then quit.
My father ordered Classics.
Every month, a new green brick,
gold trim, tiny writing.
Mom never opened them.
Auntie Charlotte read hers (the *Britannica*),
cover-to-cover, discovering eighty mistakes.
The publisher sent representatives
to consult her before the revision.

Today, phone rings bring
outsourced irritations during tea.
Door knocks solicit charity tins,
smiling solar-panel salesteens.
No one asks to come inside.
NO! still means keep talking.

Tucker's Caravan

'We were out in the Morris one day, and we passed one of those trailers, you know, a little trailer there, a box-like trailer and all of a sudden it hit me there: if we could get that trailer, take it back to the hotel there, I could build some sort of a camping arrangement on top of it. See? Because I had the Australian bent wire mentality. You could do anything with a bit of bent wire.' – Albert Tucker

In Left Bank Paris, in bedbug Paris,
the Paris, of Beats and sailors,
for an American radio and a thousand francs,
Albert Tucker bought a trailer.

Sick of rent, sick of squalor,
sick of Turkish Johns,
on that box-like trailer frame,
he saw a caravan.

He hitched it to his Morris Minor,
(the idea was absurd),
and parked down below his room,
against the hotel curb.

Right on the Rue de Verneuil,
with planks and two-by-fours,
he lengthened out the steel beard
and built a wooden floor.

The hotel owner helped him haul
materials up the flights,
inside his room, he cut the sides,
from sheets of Masonite.

Then, out the hotel window,
he lowered down each section,
down to the kerbside, to complete
and finish the erection.

Of course, it was illegal.
It broke all regulations,
but gendarmes swinging their batons
refused to write citations.

Instead, they laughed, encouraging
the mad entrepreneur:
You're making gold, there, Mr. Tucker.
Merveilleux! L'oro, monsieur!

Al screwed it all together,
and hooked it to his Morris,
then drove it past the old *clochards*,
all through the streets of Paris.

Past the old *clochards*, he drove.
He parked it near the Seine,
and lived a rent-free painter's life,
amongst the fishermen.

Blackman With Dementia

'I don't want to be logical.
I can answer all your questions,
as long as they are acute
and a bit wayward.' – Charles Blackman

An elderly man stands impossibly close,
face practically touching the canvas.
The signature red beret is tilted.
He stares up into the pigments.
Disturbances in the eyesight,
an unsteady stance and shaky gait,
are Korsakoff Syndrome,
from a lifetime of too much alcohol,
a disease once known as wet brain.
His fellow Antipodeans are dead,
Boyd and Pugh, from heart attack,
Percival, from schizophrenia and stroke.
This last one spends most afternoons sitting,
watching old James Bond films,
but his hearing is going.
The illness has brought confusion, apathy,
an inability to concentrate, and three nurses
providing twenty-four-hour care.

Now, television switched off,
the old red-capped 007 stands
motionless   in the gallery,
face practically touching the paintings.
He is again adrift in work,
playing chess with the Hatter,
sipping tea with Alice,
back in the rowboat with the Bunny.

Da Vinci Was a Bastard

'[Do not] make figures too gnarled with muscles, lest they resemble *un sacco di noci* [a sack of walnuts].' – Da Vinci, on Michaelangelo.

A hardly-mentioned talent:
improvisation on the silver lyre –
his playing surpassing
many of the court professionals
of the Duke of Milan.
Six musicians entertained
Mona Lisa Gherardini while
he painted. (Some say
her one-sided smile was a result of bruxism,
the habit of grinding one's teeth
from stress; others say
her face was his own.)

Left-handed, a vegetarian, illegitimate,
very strong (with his bare hands,
he could unbend a horseshoe).

He actively searched for bodily
deformed people to paint,
leading to his reputation
as the father of caricature.

While, temporarily, in remand,
and charged with sodomy,
he sketched a device
for opening cell doors
from the inside.

Three-ring Fleas

lived a year, three months, more likely.
With vertical leaps of seven inches, long jumps of twelve,
one out of ten was athletic enough to reach the Little Top.
In 1570, to promote meticulous craftsmanship,
blacksmiths first attached microscopic chains to torsos.
Other bugs bore golden saddles, re-enacting Waterloo.
Fleastars became sideshow-famous
amongst bearded ladies and camel girls.
They dove from platforms, walked thread,
appeared to read books, but,
ultimately untrainable,
legerdemain was employed:
glue affixed harnesses to backs, tiny fiddles to legs,
lint, on a flipped-over bug, triggered juggling.
Due to the siphonaptera's virtual invisibility,
sleight-of-handers rigged magnets, to twiddle
mini-props, simulating non-existent actors.
Improved hygiene contributed to decline in popularity,
as circus escapees often traded
plague, typhus and tapeworm.

Green Dream

Not absinthe,
or a world without global warming,
the barbiturate Nembutal,
illegally imported, mail-order, in perfume boxes,
from Mexico, Peru, Bangkok, Beijing,
Tijuana (destination of choice for death tourists),
available from local pet shops,
Holy Grail of suicide,
the peaceful pill.

Legal in Netherlands, Belgium, Switzerland and Oregon.
Promoted by end-of-life organisations Exit International, Dignitas.
Green-dyed, distinctive colour, to prevent accidental use,
created to euthanise animals.

The drug of choice for veterinarians,
at four times the rate of general population.
One took her four dogs and two cats,
before herself.

Ag

Argentum.
Seventh metal of antiquity.
Noble metal of alchemists.
Represented by crescent moon.
Less malleable than gold, high polish.
Thirty pieces sold Jesus.
Muhammad wore it on his little finger.
Da Vinci, Durer and Raphael drew with it.
Trembles in photographic film, X-rays, mirrors,
bandages, dental amalgams, catheters,
solder, infrared telescopes,
reactor control rods, solar cells,
flutes, trumpets.
The greatest of all electrical conductors.
Eatable flakes known as Vark.
Too much taken internally
produces argyria: blue skin.
Kills bacteria in vitro.
Three forms of deterioration:
black tarnish (in air),
pale yellow (in water),
purple (in light).

Dissolves in cyanide.

Chewy Blues

In fifties Ohio, when my mother
saw little me pick gum,
off the footpath, she'd yell:
Don't eat that! A coloured person
might have had that in their mouth.

A few years ago, a white singer,
supporting BB King,
was blowing bubbles, by the stage.
King came up behind her and asked
if she had any more chewy.

Embarrassed, the girl apologised, saying,
No, that was my last piece.

King said, that's okay, plucked it
out of her mouth and put it in his own.
Then he stepped up onto the stage,
smiled down at her,
and played a blistering blues set.

Close Encounters of the Blowfly Kind

In sci-fi films, Saucers
hover, then dart away,
at speeds unmatched
by any plane,
explained away, by scientists,
as technology, centuries ahead of our own.
Buzzing in front of me is a fat irritating bush fly,
wings blurred to either side, barely moving, a drone.
Without warning, it veers forty degrees
straight up, out of sight,
an impossible zigzag
too fast to follow, much less swat.
Why don't the flight engineers
study this little bastard?

Possomnia

Short, rattling, guttural,
territorial vibrato, incongruous
with that furry baby face.
Torch light cones a child's soft toy
clinging to a branch.
Brief staring match between
my beam and wide moon eyes.
An hour later, thud!
on overhead tin, claws-on-chalkboard,
thump thump, waddling
nocturnal toddler trying to find entry,
but every crack chicken-wire sealed.

Last year, sleep starved, I shot one,
eaten at midnight with potatoes.
I know, I know: protected species,
but so are humans and sleep is sacred.

This year, it's live and let rattle.
I lie awake, biting my lip,
contemplating scratch and bump.
Most eventually leave empty-fisted,
and I recall sleep, but
for the occasional stubborn cousins,
the back end of a broom handle
sends 'em scissoring off.

Cullinan

A flash of light in shaft wall.
First thought: glass. Captain Fredrick
Wells' pocketknife released the 621-gram stone,
twice the size of any before, named after the South
African mine. Remarkable clarity, save the black spot at centre
indicating internal strain. Birthday gift from Botha to Edward VII in the
presence of the Queens of Spain and Norway. Asscher, the greatest cleaver of
the day, broke a knife chipping it into three, then seven majors, ninety-six small
brilliants. Cullinan I: Great Star of Africa, pear-cut, set in the head of the Sceptre
with the Cross. Cullinan II: Second Star of Africa, rectangular-cut, soul of the
circlet of the Imperial State Crown. Cullinan III & IV: known as Lesser Stars,
pear-and-cushion-cuts, for Queen Mary's Crown (nicknamed Granny's Chips).
Cullinan V, VI & VII: heart-pear-and-marquis-cut brooch, crafted for the
stomacher of the Delhi Durbar Parue, Queen Elizabeth's favourite.
Cullinan VIII: brooch extension, never worn:
(Her Majesty claimed it got in the soup).
Cullinan IX: better behaved, four-
carat, pear-cut, set in a platinum
ring. The complete
array: one
billion
£.

Poetry Is Like Looking

Poetry is like looking
for a haystack in a needle.

A Rune of One's Own

Aching of gallstones.
Virginia Woolf's coat pockets?
Not enough to drown.

Ode To a Bush Dunny

'Je pense, donc je suis.' – Descartes

Young goanna slithers slow,
round and round the compost hole.
Mr Bellbird pings and prattles,
old cicadas shake their rattles.
Here I sit: the thinking man,
(someone call Auguste Rodin.)

Toothsome

Chaucer wrote of the gap-toothed wife of Bath,
suggesting lustful characteristics of the diastema.

Dents du bonheur. Lucky teeth.
Soldiers in Napoleon's army,
holding rifles with two hands,
required perfect incisors, for use
in opening powder magazines.
Gap-toothed men were classified unfit to fight.
Some broke theirs to avoid war.

The Passion gap, or Cape Flats smile.
South African fashion modification.
Fishermen removed the front ones
to whistle louder to one another.
Popular, for 1,500 years, it brought
beliefs of improved oral sex and kissing.
Peer pressure, and gangsterism,
made it rite of passage for poor boys.

Ohaguro, blackened teeth.
Common in ancient Japan.
Women ingested dyes of oxided iron fillings,
soaked in tea or sake, harsh taste
abetted with cinnamon, cloves, anise.
Practised amongst prostitutes, and geishas,
ohaguro signified a woman's sexual maturity.
Banned in 1870.

Joan Crawford's molars were removed on both sides.
Sunken cheeks, known as the buckle –
slang arising from dentistry, buccal.
Infected gums, and swelling, stretched her smile,
leaving a larger upper lip (which she liked), so
she painted in the lower,
creating the Crawford mouth.

Sense of Out-of-place

Barbecue.
    Unincorporated community in North Carolina.
Bastardstown.
    Townland in Wexford, Ireland (Irish name: Baile Bhastaird)
Batman.
    City, in Turkey, threatened to sue Warner Bros for use of name.
Bitch Mountain.
    Summit in Essex County, New York.
Boring, Oregon.
    Sister city to Dull, Scotland, and Bland, NSW.
Boquete.
    Small town in Panama. (*Boquete* is Portuguese slang for 'blowjob'.)
California.
    After an island, in the Spanish novel *Las Sergas de Esplandián* (1500), inhabited only by black women, ruled by Queen Calafia.
Port Circumcision.
    Cove in Petermann Island, Antarctica.
Coffin Top.
    Mountain in South Georgia.
Dead Women Crossing.
    Bridge in Custer County, Oklahoma, haunted by ghost of murdered woman.
Head-Smashed-In Buffalo Jump.
    Area in Rocky Mountain foothills.
Idiotville.
    Ghost town in Oregon.

Nowhere Else.
> Town in Tasmania.

Once Brewed and Twice Brewed.
> Two villages in Northumbria.

Ragged Ass Road.
> Street in Yellowknife, Canada.

Saint-Louis-du-Ha! Ha!
> Town in Saguenay, Quebec.

Swastika.
> 1908 mining town in northern Ontario.

Zzyzx.
> Town in California. (Also the name of a film, box office gross $30.)

I Dreamt I Saw St Augustine
(St Dominic As Well)

I dreamt I saw St Augustine
(St Dominic as well),
brothers in Christ and Light, but from
both men the shadows fell.

St Augustine was patron saint,
of brewers and of printers,
he argued for Just War Theory,
Original Sinners.

Latin was his childhood language,
a hedonistic youth,
the most sexual of all the Saints,
thieving and lust uncouth

inspired his oft repeated prayer
(soon, he'd be celibate):
Lord, please grant me chastity and
continence…but not yet!

His arguments against magic
formed the core decisions,
for persecution of witches,
during the Inquisition.

I dreamt I saw St Augustine
(St Dominic as well),
brothers in Christ and Light, but in
both men the shadows fell.

St Domenic's Dominicans,
Pope Innocent adored.
A play on *Dominicanus* –
Latin: Dog of the Lord.

St Dominic's advice was sought
to root out the Cathars,
the only Crusade within the faith,
a Christian civil war.

A score of years in Southern France
to put heretics down,
a victory apparent but
the Cathars went to ground

and practised outlawed beliefs to
the Feminine above,
with songs to Ladies of the Crown,
in veiled Courtly Love.

St Domenic's lost troubadours,
romantic harbingers,
through musing Ladies of the Court,
presaged our folksingers.

I dreamt I saw St Augustine
(St Dominic as well),
brothers in Christ and Light, but on
both men the shadows fell.

An Interesting Little Girl

An interesting little girl, The Argus read.

Further down,
…hearing she was seriously ill,
I volunteered to ride to Melbourne…

At a schoolhouse, gathering, May 18th 1851,
…a full congregation of settlers heard the service…
…but the Reverend P. Gunn had to leave for another engagement…

An urgent need for somewhere to put her,
became Kangaroo Ground Cemetery,
…as her mother put it,
'she caught a chill from resting on wet grass'…

Five-year-old Judith Furphy was dearly loved,
youngest sister of John,
wheelwright, inventor
of the Furphy Water Cart (at Gallipoli),

and Joseph,
father of the Australian novel,
who, in 1903, under pen name, wrote
Such is Life.

Little Blue Book

We were both eleven or twelve,
shared desks at St Mary's Bible study class,
reading our little blue Catechism books.

One time he dragged me in a brown wagon
across town, straight
down the centre of a dangerous
five-lane intersection, somehow
avoiding whizzing traffic.

My mother was waiting for me,
at our front gate, holding
the wooden pasta spoon that spoke
when words weren't enough.

A few weeks later, he didn't come to Bible study.
I watched his empty desk,
as the nun told us he had been hit
by a car and killed on his way to class.
She said the last thing he said
to the ambulance attendant was

Where is my blue book?

Three months after the burial,
the empty desk filled,
I heard his father, struck
with grief, had shot himself,
through the mouth, with a shotgun,
over the small grave.

Lyrics

The Green-eyed Boy of the Rain

Somehow we drifted into this wet place
I just couldn't feel any pain
he came and stole her away from me
the green-eyed boy of the rain.

I wanted to kill him to tear him apart
until nothing of him would remain
when I thought of him kissing her mouth
the green-eyed boy of the rain.

I thought I had rights to her body and soul
now I can't even say her name
I drove her away and right into the arms of
the green-eyed boy of the rain.

Anger and sorrow become the same thing
two sides of a dark windowpane
I'd give everything to see her look back from
the green-eyed boy of the rain.

The Ballad of the Gangster Paul Kelly

Quiet down children and please pay heed to me
I'll tell you about Paul Kelly who was born in Sicily
in eighteen hundred and ninety he came to New York town
his Five Point Gang took control of the criminal underground.

Born Paolo Antonio Vaccarelli he changed his name
when he immigrated from Italy pro boxing was his game
he took his fighting money and put it into whores
ran them in the Bowery and on the docks and shores.

Now the Irish gangs were dominant in the New York railway yards
the Ducky Boys, Dead Rabbits, Swamp Angels and Roach Guards.
Paul Kelly ushered in the rise of mixed-ethnic crews
he took them all: Italians Poles Russians and the Jews.

He recruited younger gangsters who later became renown
Meyer Lansky, Lucky Luciano, Bugsy Siegel and Al Capone
he spent nine months in jail for assault and robbery
spoke English French Italian and Spanish fluently.

Paul Kelly was well-dressed sophisticated – a learned mind
endeared him to the socialites and politicians of the time
known as Gentleman Mob Boss on Lower Manhattan streets
his Little Naples nightclub was the in-crowd place to meet.

Now the dearest rivals to the Five Points Gang to come along
were Max Eastman's Coin Collectors two thousand gunmen strong
Max Eastman was a jewish bouncer and hired thug to boot
so a boxing match was arranged to settle their turf dispute.

Kelly and Eastman fought it out but it ended in a draw
a war broke out that was only settled by intercession of the Law
ten long years in Sing Sing forced Max Eastman to retreat
which left Paul Kelly undisputed mob boss of the streets.

So quiet down now children and please pay heed to me
I'll tell you about Paul Kelly who was born in Sicily
in eighteen hundred and ninety he came to New York town
his Five Point Gang took control of the criminal underground.

Transportation To America

William Henry was caught
stealing bread from a cart
seven years he got
transportation to America

for the crime of being poor
he was shackled to the floor
of an British man-o'-war
transportation to America

many a shirtback was ripped
for the cat-o'-nine whip
to the colonies they were shipped
transportation to America

there indentured as slaves
many met early graves
for the prison space they'd save
transportation to America

oh the sentence of gravest threat
that a prisoner could expect
short of hanging by the neck
transportation to America

during the Colonial War
Mr John Hancock swore
they'd be taking no more
transportation to America

where to put the convict waste?
then Lord Sydney made his case
New South Wales could replace
transportation to America.

Black Caesar: the First Bushranger

John Caesar fled to England from plantation slavery
born in Madagascar or West Indies – it wasn't clear
tried and then convicted in Kent for petty theft
shipped to the penal colony in New South Wales for seven years

Caesar! Hail Caesar! Black Caesar was his name
transported by the First Fleet in chains to Botany Bay
escaped with just a musket from the jailer's whip and rack
come hear ye all Australians – the first bushranger was black

Black Caesar plundered farms and huts on outskirts of the towns
his frame was strong muscular well-calculated for hard work
reputed to be the hardest living convict in the Crown
five gallons of rum was offered by the Governor for his return

Now Pemulwuy an aboriginal of the Bidjigal clan
attacked John Caesar and his crew one night in Botany Bay
seven pellets of lead buckshot lodged in that warrior's skull
but Caesar only grazed him and Pemulwuy got away

sly Caesar was indifferent about meeting his own death
at the threat of hanging by the neck the convict merely scoffed
he bragged he'd play a trick upon the executioner
and create a laugh for all who watched before he was turned off

John Wimbow and another man allured by the reward
found his haunt and concealed themselves in brush behind a shed
in the morning Caesar emerged but before he sensed the threat
John Wimbow fired his musket there and shot the convict dead

Caesar! Hail Caesar! Black Caesar was his name
transported by the First Fleet in chains to Botany Bay
escaped with just a musket from the jailer's whip and rack
come hear ye all Australians – the first bushranger was black.

Harry Power: the Last Bushranger

Gather round me children and hear my tale
sit with me for an hour
and I'll tell you the story of the last bushranger
by the name of Harry Power.

Harry was broad-shouldered in his oilskin coat
in his grey beard he looked older
with a double-barrelled shotgun in his good right hand
in his left a muzzle-loader.

Harry Power turned a fugitive
when he escaped from Pentridge gaol
he fled to his gunyah in the King River Valley
with the troopers on his trail.

Harry robbed the house of a Christian woman
she started to read him her Bible
he said save it for those sods that are still in Pentridge
give me your money and the silver on your table.

By Eleven Mile Creek he passed one day
and uttering hardly a sentence
he took the young Ned Kelly away
to take him for his apprentice.

Ned Kelly was but fourteen years old
but his mother she approved
go with Harry Power Ned said she
for the father you hardly knew.

Harry bailed up old Robert Mcbean
a wealthy squatter from Benalla
he stole his horse his saddle his bridle
and a gold watch that he valued.

Harry asked a mate by the name of Jack Lloyd
to act as go-between
to return the gold watch for fifteen pounds
in a deal with squatter McBean.

The Chief of Police a Captain Standish
approached this Judas Jack Lloyd
and persuaded him inform on the old bushranger
for the five-hundred-pound reward.

Jack Lloyd led those outlaw hunters
up the mountain spur so steep
on a starry night they found Harry's camp
and they took him in his sleep.

Harry Power was startled but he wasn't dismayed
he said I guess I was careless
but you boys look hungry so sit back awhile
and he cooked those coppers their breakfast.

Harry was remanded to Wangaratta
where the crowds came out and cheered
but the judge returned him to Pentridge prison
for a further fifteen years.

Harry served his time and he was released
with seven pounds to his name
he had been in prisons almost half his life
he was sixty-six years of age.

Harry's final years were spent as a guide
on the prison hulk Success
the very same ship where he'd had once been a convict
now a museum for the tourists.

Old Harry drowned in the Murray River
while off fishing alone
the last of the Golden Bushrangers was gone
and his grave remains unknown,

so gather round me children and hear my tale
sit with me for an hour
and I'll tell you the story of the last bushranger
by the name of Harry Power.

Dry Whisky Tongue

Bring me scotch whisky for my dry whisky tongue
your wine is much too tame
your wine is much too tame

an old girl to kiss my dry whisky tongue
Laphroaig is her name
Miss Laphroaig is her name

six weeks of drought with a dry whisky tongue
I need some whisky rain
I need some whisky rain

your tears will not quench my dry whisky tongue
saltwater ain't the same
saltwater just ain't the same

I woke in a sweat with a dry whisky tongue
that little whisky ghost
was jumping in my brain

if I go blind with my dry whisky tongue
send a whisky dog
to guide home my aim

if surely I must die with a dry whisky tongue
place some whisky flowers
down there by my name.

Mr Critical

They call me Mr Critical
Mr Critical is my name
I can find the flaw in a feather
the crack in a drop of rain.

I've been granted authority
by the Holy Whatchamacallit
all you Masters of Shovelling Shit
I be the one to haul it
and all your mighty Engines of Wit
I be the one to stall it

I was born under a baldhead moon
I sucked on a milkless breast
whooped with a barbwire rattle
my dolly was a hornet's nest

I run off my teachers with a two-handed axe
I burned my school to the ground
if I don't know it, it can't be known
and now I'll tell you how.

Call me Mr Critical
Mr Critical is my name
I can find the flaw in a feather
the crack in a drop of rain.

Mr Q

Friday was the day new comics came out
Superman Green Lantern and *The Flash*
down to Mr Q's comic book shop
we ten-year-old kids would all dash

while I was reading squatting in the aisle
Mr Q would come up behind
press himself against me there
rubbing his cheek against mine

he'd give me a squeeze and ask how I was
then he'd start playing with my hair
I'd tell him I was fine and continue reading
pretending he just wasn't there

I thought Mr Q was like those relatives
the kind that always try to kiss you
even when you don't much feel like doing it
but your folks tell you that you just have to

Mr Q
what happened to you?
I heard you got busted
I guess you couldn't be trusted
man you were so creepy too

a few of my friends told me Mr Q
sometimes would take them downstairs
and give them ten dollars to let him play with them
but that was something I never dared

don't get me wrong I thought about it
when Mr Q would give me those looks
ten whole dollars back in those days
bought a lot of comic books

Mr Q
what happened to you?
I heard you got busted
I guess you couldn't be trusted
man you were so creepy too.

Out of Book

for Chris Depasquale

You look at your position and you see the trap
your clock's running down and you can't go back
looking for some strategy that's sane
you're wondering if you sacrifice just what you'd gain.

Forget the theories from the book
close your eyes and take another look
it's no longer black and white once again
welcome back to where you've never been.

You're still dizzy from your success
you can't tell the good moves from the best
the king's in the castle face down on the throne
your queen is starting to feel just like a guest.

A black pawn puts the question to your good bishop:
are you going to take something leave or just remain?
You'd like more time just to analyse this line
because you know it's a struggle and not a game.

Forget the theories from the book
close your eyes and take another look
it's no longer black and white once again
welcome back to where you've never been.

The Awful Flanders and Wallonia Train Wreck

The rumour spread quickly as commuters gathered round
one train had left Halle Station and was travelling northern bound
the other was the local from Buizingen headed down

for a fateful meeting on the Brussels–Mons track
in that awful Flanders and Wallonia train wreck.

The carriages were compacted together by the crash
brute force had caused the power lines above to be detached
survivors staggered out amongst dead bodies on the tracks

the driver of the southern train killed instantly on deck
in the awful Flanders and Wallonia train wreck.

A spokesman for the government said nineteen people died
another fifty badly injured more were hospitalised
some said one train had run the red or on the wrong line

others blamed ice even the driver was suspect
in the awful Flanders and Wallonia train wreck.

Wallonia had the country's highest unemployment rate
Flanders was resigned to vote Secession as its fate
the split would be the final straw for Belgium as a state

but that day all Belgians felt the loss and the regret
of the awful Flanders and Wallonia train wreck.

Dead Cat Bounce

for Peter Marks

When your blue chip is starting to look much bluer
and your speculative has just lost its life
and you buying in at the bottom
is like trying to catch a falling knife
your dollar is more expensive by the hour
your gold is getting cheaper by the ounce
you're calling every twitch a rebound
friend, it's the Dead Cat Bounce.

Well, nobody is buying what you're selling
because nobody can hear you shout
your broker is turning into your joker
and your tipsters are all tiptoeing out
the bull has bolted the paddock
and the bear is just about to pounce
you're seeing half-full when it's really half-empty
friend, it's the Dead Cat Bounce.

Your paper has lost all its profit
and your Gordon Gekko has finally been caught
the tulips are looking like stinkweed
and your dot.com has lost all its dot
Elvis has long left the building
the fat lady is all sung out
all your dogs aren't having their days
friend, it's the Dead Cat Bounce.

Well, you'd like to cut all your losses
but there ain't a whole lot left to cut
you're thinking it's better to hold them than fold them
but soon you'll be holding your butt
you're just waiting for that big announcement
for some reason they just won't announce
when even the banks are starting to look good
friend, it's the Dead Cat Bounce.

Everything Is Fixed

after Bob Dylan

Fixed lips and fixed skin
fixed nose and a fixed chin
fixed preachers and fixed sin
fixed politicians with fixed kin

> you can teach a new dog old tricks
> everything is fixed

fixed tips from a fixed source
fixed stocks on a fixed bourse
fixed punch and a fixed horse
fixed grades in a fixed course

> my heart's been hurt by stones and sticks
> everything is fixed

they say new things don't last like the old
but even old money is losing control
superglue band aides staples duct tape
all going to shake in a 9 Richter quake

> if it ain't broke it can still be fixed
> everything is fixed

fixed ceilings and fixed doors
fixed news and fixed wars
fixed banks and fixed boards
fixed charts and fixed awards

> so much patching is giving me ticks
> everything is fixed.

I Never Found Those Lips Again

I never found those lips again
my final preference for her kiss
I never thought that I could bend

when she had gone it felt the end
sorrow broke open an abyss
I never found those lips again

kind words from a few mutual friends
who didn't vanish into mist
I never thought that I could bend

some lovers with a soft pretend
their touch somehow always amiss
I never found those lips again

the helpful advice that offends
(there still too much I won't dismiss)
I never thought that I could bend

an almost heal but never mend
the unannounced recall of bliss
I never found those lips again
I never thought that I could bend.

Jean La Pucelle

I was just thirteen,
When the voices came to me,
I was tending father's sheep,
Down by the village stream.

I saw a mighty vision,
My head held to the ground.
I heard the sound of angels,
Some were winged, and some were crowned.

My mind received impressions,
As angels spoke to me:
Daughter of God, now you must go,
By your side, I shall be.

Raise a Holy Army,
Fight a Holy War.
The angels, thus, commanded me,
And led me to the sword.

The light within the spirit of man,
Is equal to the light,
Within the spirit of woman,
Both equal, in God's sight.

I neither acted a woman,
Nor talked as women talked,
I wore the clothes of soldiers,
And walked as soldiers walked.

I rode the strongest horses,
I had knowledge of the Amazon,
I was wounded in the breast, by arrows,
But continued to fight on.

My picture was put in churches,
When I freed my native land,
Medals were struck in my image,
Followers kissed my hand.

I was then sorely accused,
Of magic, they dictated,
Bound and tried, at a trial of faith,
And excommunicated.

They said I invoked demons,
Of a relapsed heretic,
But I was caught up in the lime,
Of church politics.

They shaved my head and burned me,
My loyal soldiers wept,
It's said they saw, with dying breaths,
A dove rise from my breast.

Lullaby Redux

rock a bye baby on the tree top
poor little baby's high as a cat
send for the chap in the fireman's hat
to put up a ladder or give it a chop

when the wind blows the cradle will rock
clouds will just whimper the moon start to talk
branches will shake and all the leaves drop
to fill up your cradle right to the top

when the bough breaks the cradle will fall
scraping the branches on the way down
baby comes tumbling spinning around
mommy will cry and daddy will call

down will come baby cradle and all
daddy will catch you in his strong arms
mommy can hide you away from all harm
and wrap you up tight in a swaddling shawl.

In the Next Life

Sometimes I think about my mother,
the way she used to hold me tight,
I know she's waiting for me there,
in the next life.

It's been so long since I saw him,
so many things we didn't put right.
Father and son will speak together,
in the next life.

There's no need to feel so angry,
there's no need for us to fight,
the puzzle's pieces will all fit,
in the next life.

from The Leadbelly Ballad Novel

Jack Johnson and the Mann Act

There's a Rembrandt on the wall
of the Cabaret de Champions
purchased by Jack Johnson
when he boxed overseas

a portrait of Jack Johnson
and his white wife by Clarkson
in oils of black and white
for all the world to see.

The greatest fighter of that time
was a black man named Jack Johnson
he defeated every single
White Hope they could find.

The white folks used to riot
at the gall of that uppity Negro
the supremacy of the white race
was riding on the line.

They done him wrong
they didn't want Jack Johnson's kind around
so they had to use the Mann Act of 1910
to finally bring him down.

The Mann Act was written
in the early nineteen hundreds
to stop the transportation
of whores across state lines

designed to catch white slavers
it soon became a handy tool
of the crooked politicians
and their personal designs.

The lowest blow was struck
on the suicide of his dear wife
his enemies surrounded him
and drew out their sharp knives

a white girl named Belle Schreiber
the daughter of a policeman
testified that Jack Johnson
took her across state lines.

They done him wrong
they didn't want Jack Johnson around
so they had to use the Mann Act of 1910
to finally bring him down.

Give Me Little Sugar With My Beer Sylvie

Give me little sugar with my beer Sylvie
give me little sugar with my beer
it's a bitter taste but I'll drink a case
if you give me little sugar with my beer.

Huddie met two girls dancing
they both were fine high browns
they asked him where he came from
he said Chicago town.

Those two girls started jiving him
he was only fourteen years old
daddy won't you take us way up town
and buy us some beer that's cold?

Huddie ordered up two glasses
then he ordered up one more
he filled his mouth and swallowed down
then he spat it on the floor.

Oh daddy, you from Chicago
but you can't hold your beer.
Huddie said no I can't drink it straight
unless you bring me little sugar over here.

Give me little sugar with my beer Sylvie
give me little sugar with my beer
it's a bitter taste but I'll drink a case
if you give me little sugar with my beer.

Marie Laveau La Belle Voodooienne

Marie Laveau *la mère* was mulatto
she married Jacque Paris a quadroon
her curly black hair reddish skin and good looks
made her the queen of Orleans voudoun.

In rituals on Bayou St John
Marie danced with her snake Zombi
a friend to the Marquis de Lafayette
in the town of Old Orleans.

> *Oh Marie Laveau eh bien!*
> *Oh Marie la belle voodooienne.*

When her husband Jacque disappeared
she became the Widow Paris
and bore fifteen children to Christoph Glapion
a quadroon from Saint Dominique.

The Creole women of Orleans
would come to mamzel Laveau
to confide their intimate secrets and fears
of their husbands their business and their souls.

The Orleans white masters feared her
with her African gibberish and stare
resolutions were passed confining her dance
to the place know as Congo Square

but the whites of every class still sought her
even judges would pay for her spells
for Marie Laveau was the queen of voodoo
and her *gris-gris* could make sick things well.

Marie Laveau was more than a witch
she practised Catholicism
with prayers incense and statues of saints
nursed the sick the diseased and the condemned.

Now resting in St Louis Cemetery
sits the crypt of mamzel Marie
three crosses in red brick dust on the stone vault
grants a wish for those who believe.

> *Oh Marie Laveau eh bien!*
> *Oh Marie la belle voodooienne.*

The Happiest Times I Ever Had
(Was Whoo! Playin' the Blues)

Having the blues and playing the blues
are two diffcrent kinds of news
the happiest times I ever had
      was whoo! playin' the blues.

Now don't ask me to explain
'cause I ain't got no clues
the happiest times I ever had
      was whoo! playin' the blues.

I don't wish you to get blues
'cause having them don't amuse
the happiest times I ever had
      was whoo! playin' the blues.

Sometimes the blues can kill you
'bout break you in twos
the happiest times I ever had
      was whoo! playin' the blues.

The blues get you in the morning
your whole day be confused
the happiest times I ever had
      was whoo! playin' the blues.

Sometime the blues are discouragin'
everything you do you lose
the happiest times I ever had
      was whoo! playin' the blues.

The blues don't give no warning
they sure don't follow no rules
the happiest times I ever had
        was whoo! playin' the blues.

The blues wear out your mind
and the leather in your shoes
the happiest times I ever had
        was whoo! playin' the blues.

The blues will make you act primitive
like the monkeys in the zoos
the happiest times I ever had
        was whoo! playin' the blues.

The blues can make you hateful
and turn your brain to stews
the happiest times I ever had
        was whoo! playin' the blues.

They don't get happy with drugs
they don't get happy with booze
the happiest times I ever had
        was whoo! playin' the blues.

The blues can paint your heart
in every shade and hues
the happiest times I ever had
        was whoo! playin' the blues.

The pain can melt you down
but you can break it like a fuse
the happiest times I ever had
          was whoo! playin' the blues.

You have to have 'em to play 'em
but having them can abuse
the happiest times I ever had
          was whoo! playin' the blues.

Jelly With My Cake Blues

Knock me out a kiss give me jelly with my cake
knock me out a kiss give me jelly with my cake
it must be jelly because jam sure don't shake

you don't know what's shaking until you come shake my tree
you don't know what's shaking until you come shake my tree
I'm the best moaner daddy that you will ever see

I don't need no monkey woman to give me the Hateful Blues
I don't need no monkey woman to give me the Hateful Blues
just give me some jelly the kind I can't refuse

don't be mistreating me like my last man do
don't be mistreating me like my last man do
if I catch you cheatin' me I'm gonna cheat on you

I got a sugarfoot I got a pigfoot too
I got a sugarfoot I got a pigfoot too
it's got to be jelly because jam just won't do

knock me out a kiss give me jelly with my cake
knock me out a kiss give me jelly with my cake
it must be jelly because jam sure don't shake.

Lead

Lead is the oldest metal
connected to the planet Saturn
some pipes still bear the inscription
of Roman emperors.

Sugar of lead was used in Rome
as sweetener for wine
and said to cause dementia
in several emperors' minds.

Pencil lead isn't lead at all
graphite is used instead
but the Roman stylus the *pencillus*
was fashioned out of lead.

Lead resists corrosion
and is easy to extract
lead is used with antimony
mixed with arsenic.

Alchemists respected lead
the toxin and sure poison
lead in toys and paints has caused
the deaths of countless children.

Lead is bluest when first cut
and tarnishes in air
when mixed in part with brass
reduces machine tool wear.

Lead is part of solder
used for pewter pots
lead is poured for bullet weight
lead is cast for shot.

The symbol Pb signifies
the Latin root plumbum
gave the English word plumbing
when lead pipes were the custom.

Pig Tails In Gravy

Pig tails in gravy ain't that hard to cook
remember this song and you
won't need your recipe book

two pounds of tails for a pig tail treat
cut each pig tail into three or four piece
one large onion a stalk of celery
chop it coarsely as coarse as it can be

four cups water quarter cup of vinegar
add onions celery pig tails and stir
black pepper salt teaspoon of chili flakes
cover and simmer – takes an hour to make

Pig tails in gravy ain't that hard to cook
remember this song and you
won't need your recipe book

preheat the oven take the tails from the broth
bake 'em at 350° until the fat browns off
third cup of flour a third of water too
mix to a paste and stir until smooth

stir up the flour paste into the broth
stir it until the gravy gets smooth and soft
put the tails in the gravy simmer low heat
in fifteen minutes check your seasoning and eat

Pig tails in gravy ain't that hard to cook
remember this song and you
won't need your recipe book.

Red Velvet Cake

I don't need no smothered pork chops
I don't need no T-bone steak
just give me another portion
of that Red Velvet Cake

I don't need no crackling corn bread
I don't need no shake & bake
just give me some pecan frosting
on that Red Velvet Cake

now don't slip in red food colouring
god knows we don't need a fake
just squeeze a little fresh beet juice
in the Red Velvet Cake

sunrise is red in the morning
sunset is red on the lake
but there ain't no red half as red
as your Red Velvet Cake.

Houston Riot of 1917

Gentlemen and generals, members of the Bar,
I ask you to hear and review the facts just as they are,
in the matter of this riot and soldiers mutiny,
of the Third Battalion, 24th black US Infantry.

The boys were sent to Houston, from free New Mexico,
under orders from the War Department telling them to go,
but the segregated Texans denied equality,
they saw black soldiers as a threat to racial harmony.

Two hundred Negro soldiers refused the Jim Crow stamp.
A mob of angry citizens approached Fort Houston camp.
Sergeant Vida Henry, of First Company,
marched against the angry mob to quell insurgency.

A violent encounter shattered Houston's peace.
Black soldiers killed fifteen armed whites including four police.
Martial Law was declared, the 24th relieved,
seven soldiers testified in exchange for clemency.

So gentlemen, I rest my case in this court martialling,
I beg Your Honours grant acquittal and judge impartially.
Even President Wilson spoke out, but old Jim Crow couldn't hear,
thirteen black soldiers hung that Christmas – six more by New Year.

Eli Whitney and the Cotton Gin

Eli Whitney
with hammer and tin
one night invented
the cotton gin

inspired he said
by barnyard events
when a tomcat tried to pull
a chicken through the fence.

Now a cotton gin's
just a big old box
with a wire screen
and some wire hooks

in one end a cotton boll
gets pulled and cleaned
and out from the other
comes a pair of your old blue jeans.

Now some folks claim
Whitney stole that thing
from his landlady by the name
of Catherine Green

she gave him the Idea
with a hairbrush and a pin
but women weren't allowed
to have patents way back then.

Historians believe
that the cotton gin
was the key to the whole
damn slave system

well if we could change time
and maybe just go back
to rescue that chicken
from that old tomcat

or hide Mrs Green's brush
under the floor
we might have prevented
the Civil War

and Abraham Lincoln
wouldn't have been shot
the Battle of Gettysburg
might not have been fought

no slavery
no plantations
no Ku Klux Klan
no segregation

and Eli Whitney
with his hammer and tin
might have just had to settle
for inventing the garbage bin.

Lafayette's Mixture

I was terrible with women
I was terrible rough
I just treat them every which way
sometimes I just throw them off.

I had trainloads of women
I had daughters I had the mothers
if they wouldn't go with me
I'd go find me another.

Surely don't need no doctor
surely don't need no pill
just give me some Lafayette's Mixture
to cure my serious ill.

During the American Revolution
the Marquis de Lafayette
mixed a powder in a solution
to cure anything you could get.

Some people called it the pox
some folks called it the drip
the doctor calls it the gonorrhea
and it certainly made me sick.

Six weeks of suffering
six weeks of laying in bed
six weeks of Lafayette's Mixture
until you can hardly raise your head.

Surely don't need no doctor
surely don't need no pill
just give me some Lafayette's Mixture
to cure my serious ill.

Gideon Bible

Gideon was a judge of Bible lore
whom God commanded: Gideon make thou war!
Go and set the Israelites free
from their false idolatry
and while you're at it leave a Bible in the drawer.

There's a Gideon Bible in your hotel room
in this time of great uncertainty and gloom
for any sin which you are liable
just consult your Gideon Bible
in the top drawer of the dresser in your room.

Since 1908 they've been placed and read
in every hotel hospital prison cell and shed
if you stray into Satan's Lair
you'll find Gideon waiting there
in the top drawer of the dresser near your bed.

Now Gideon's name means Mighty Feller of Trees
and in that name there's a mighty prophecy
because the amount of trees it took
for all the paper in those books
I'm surprised there's any forests left for you and me.

There's a Gideon Bible in your hotel room
in this time of great uncertainty and gloom
for any sin which you are liable
just consult your Gideon Bible
in the top drawer of the dresser in your room.

Orpheo Don't Look Back

Please keep your word to me Orpheo
keep your promise and your pact
I'm right behind you Orpheo
Orpheo don't look back

I need to know you trust me Orpheo
and that I can trust you back
I'm right behind you Orpheo
Orpheo don't look back

Hold me fast and faithfully Orpheo
love's such a narrow track
I'm right behind you Orpheo
Orpheo don't look back

Imagine love forever Orpheo
a love that would never lack
I'm right behind you Orpheo
Orpheo don't look back

When souls are filled with darkness Orpheo
and light is but a crack
I'm right behind you Orpheo
Orpheo don't look back

When voices are dry as dust Orpheo
and throats with thirst are so wracked
I'm right behind you Orpheo
Orpheo don't look back.

When every fibre in your body Orpheo
says there's nothing there but black
I'm right behind you Orpheo
Orpheo don't look back.

About the author

Joe Dolce was born in the US in 1947 and moved to Australia in 1979, becoming a citizen and a dual national. Singer, songwriter, composer and poet, he is known internationally as the writer and performer of the most successful Australian song in history, 'Shaddap You Face'. He is the writer of the US country & bluegrass standard, 'My Home Ain't in the Hall of Fame'. He co-founded with Lin van Hek, his partner of thirty-seven years, the literary-music two-hander *Difficult Women*, touring for fifteen years, and performing over fifty shows at the Edinburgh Festival, with shows in Okinawa, Japan, Estonia, Canada and the UK. 'Intimacy', a song he and van Hek wrote together, was part of the soundtrack of the iconic hit movie *The Terminator*, directed by James Cameron, now part of the US Library of Congress archives.

His poetry appeared in *Best Australian Poems 2015* and *2014*. He won First Prize in the University of Canberra Health Poetry Contest 2017. He was shortlisted for the 2014 Newcastle Poetry Prize. He had two poems shortlisted in the 2017 Philip Bacon Ekphrasis Award. He was longlisted for the Canberra Vice-Chancellor's Poetry Prize in 2017 and 2014. He was the winner of the 25th Launceston Poetry Cup. His poems, essays and short stories have been published in *Meanjin*, *Monthly*, *Southerly*, *Cordite*, *The Canberra Times*, *Quadrant*, *Australian Poetry Journal*, *Verity La*, *Overland*, *Contrappasso*, *Not Shut Up* (UK) and *Antipodes* (US). From 2016 to 2017, he was on staff of the Australian Institute of Music, teaching Composition, Ensemble and Personal Tutoring in setting lyrics and poetry to music. He is a recipient of the Advance Australia Award.

www.ingramcontent.com/pod-product-compliance
Lightning Source LLC
Chambersburg PA
CBHW071824080526
44589CB00012B/908